JAMESTOWN  EDUCATION

WORLD WORKS™

LEVEL F

FOOD

NATURE

TECHNOLOGY

McGraw Hill Glencoe

New York, New York   Columbus, Ohio   Chicago, Illinois   Woodland Hills, California

JAMESTOWN EDUCATION

 Glencoe

The McGraw-Hill Companies

Send all inquiries to:
Glencoe/McGraw-Hill
130 E. Randolph Street, Suite 400
Chicago, IL 60601

ISBN: 978-0-07-878019-6
MHID: 0-07-878019-5

Printed in the United States of America.

3 4 5 6 7 8 9 10 HSO 11 10

Contents

2

Unit Two NATURE

40

78

Unit Three TECHNOLOGY

To the Student

This book has nine articles that explain how things work or how things are made. In Unit One, you'll read about food. In Unit Two, you'll learn about nature. And in Unit Three, you'll find out about technology.

The articles in this book will make you think. Some of the information in the text may amaze or even shock you. And each article is sure to improve your understanding of how the world works.

As you read this book, you will have the chance to practice six reading skills:

Making Predictions   **Asking Questions**
Making Connections   **Understanding Line Graphs**
Visualizing   **Drawing Conclusions**

Each lesson in Unit One and Unit Two will focus on one of these reading skills. In Unit Three, each lesson will focus on several of the skills at once.

You will also complete reading comprehension, vocabulary, and writing activities. Many of the activities are similar to the ones on state and national tests. Completing the activities can help you get ready for tests you may have to take later.

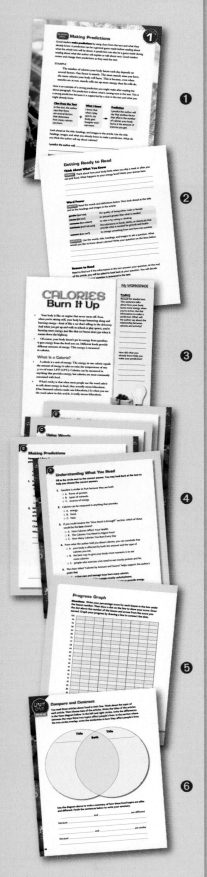

How to Use This Book

About the Book

This book has three units. Each unit has three lessons. Each lesson is built around an article about how something works or how something is made. All the articles have before-reading and after-reading activities.

Working Through Each Lesson

❶ **Reading Skill** Start each lesson by learning a reading skill and getting ready to use it.

❷ **Think About What You Know, Word Power, Reason to Read** Prepare to read the article by completing the activities on this page.

❸ **Article** Read about how something works or how something is made. Enjoy! The activities in the margins will remind you to use the reading skills.

❹ **Activities** Complete activities A, B, C, and D. Then check your work. Your teacher will give you an answer key to do this. Record the number of your correct answers for each activity. At the end of the lesson, add up your total score for activities A, B, and C. Then figure out your percentage score.

❺ **Progress Graph** Record your percentage score on the Progress Graph on page 121.

❻ **Compare and Contrast** Complete the Compare and Contrast activity at the end of each unit. The activity will help you see how the things you read about are alike and different.

Unit 1

Food

Calories

Popcorn

Genetically Modified Food

CALORIES
Burn It Up

butter
1 tablespoon
102 calories

potato
medium, baked
161 calories

chicken breast
4 oz., grilled
180 calories

asparagus
6 spears
20 calories

The energy you get
from the food you eat
is measured in calories.

READING SKILL Making Predictions

Good readers **make predictions** by using clues from the text and what they already know. A prediction can be a general guess made before reading about what the whole text will be about. A prediction can also be a guess made during reading about what the author will explain or talk about next. Good readers review and change their predictions as they read the text.

EXAMPLE

The number of calories your body burns each day depends on several factors. One factor is muscle. The more muscle mass you have, the more calories your body will burn. This is because, even when muscles are at rest, muscle cells use up more energy than fat cells do.

Here is an example of a strong prediction you might make after reading the above paragraph. The prediction is about what's coming next in the text. This is a strong prediction because it is supported by a clue in the text and what you might already know.

Clue from the Text	**What I Know**	**Prediction**
In the text, the author says that there are several factors that determine how many calories you burn.	I know that when I play sports, my body gets hungrier and I eat more.	I predict the author will say that another factor that affects the number of calories your body burns is the amount of exercise you get.

Look ahead at the title, headings, and images in the article. Use the title, headings, images, and what you already know to make a prediction. What do you think the author will say about calories?

I predict the author will _____

_____

because _____

_____

At the end of the article, you will be asked about your prediction. You will need to explain how your prediction is the same as the text or different from it.

Getting Ready to Read

Think About What You Know

CONNECT   Think about how your body feels when you skip a meal or after you eat junk food. What happens to your energy level? Write your answer here.

_____

_____

_____

Word Power

PREVIEW   Read the words and definitions below. Then look ahead at the title and at the headings and images in the article.

gender (jen′-dər)	the quality of being either male or female
excess (ek′-ses′)	an amount greater than what is needed
consume (kən-soom′)	to take in by eating or drinking
nutrients (noo′-trē-ənts)	the substances in foods, drinks, or chemicals that provide what is needed for growth and health
convert (kən-vərt′)	to change something from one form into another

QUESTION   Use the words, title, headings, and images to ask a question. What would you like to know about calories? Write your question on the lines below.

_____

_____

_____

Reason to Read

Read to find out if the information in the text answers your question. At the end of the article, you will be asked to look back at your question. You will decide whether or not your question is answered in the text.

CALORIES
Burn It Up

1   Your body is like an engine that never turns off. Even when you're sitting still, your body keeps humming along and burning energy—kind of like a car that's idling in the driveway. And when you get up and walk to school or play sports, you're burning more energy, just like that car burns more gas when it zooms down the highway.

2   Of course, your body doesn't get its energy from gasoline; it gets energy from the food you eat. Different foods provide different amounts of energy. This energy is measured in calories.

What Is a Calorie?

3   A calorie is a unit of energy. The energy in one calorie equals the amount of energy it takes to raise the temperature of one **gram** of water 1.8°F (1.0°C). Calories can be measured in anything that provides energy, but calories are most commonly associated with food.

4   What's tricky is that when most people use the word *calorie* to talk about energy in food, they actually mean kilocalorie. (One thousand calories make one kilocalorie.) So when you see the word *calorie* in this article, it really means kilocalorie.

---

gram (gram) a unit used to measure weight; a small paper clip weighs about one gram

My WORKSPACE

Predict

Reread the shaded text. This sentence talks about how your body burns more energy when you're active. Use this information to make a prediction. What will the author say about the relationship between calories and activity?

_____

_____

_____

_____

How did what you already know help you make your prediction?

_____

_____

_____

_____

The calories in a piece of cheesecake contain enough energy to light a 60-watt bulb for about an hour and a half. **Think about the energy cheesecake gives you when you eat it.**

How Much Is Enough?

5   Even if you stay in bed all day and do absolutely nothing, your body still burns a lot of calories. This is because your brain, heart, lungs, and other organs never stop working. Of all the calories you burn throughout the day, about 60 to 70 percent are used just to keep these organs functioning and to regulate your body temperature. And you burn another 10 percent of your calories just to digest your food! The remaining calories (about 20 to 30 percent) are used to fuel your muscle movements—everything from playing sports to bending over to pick up a piece of paper. (If you want to learn more about exercise, read *World Works, Level E*, Lesson 8.)

Predict

After you have read **paragraphs 6** and **7**, look back at the prediction you wrote on page 5. Does your prediction match the information in the text? Why or why not?

_____

_____

_____

_____

_____

6   The total number of calories a person burns each day depends on factors such as his or her **gender,** age, and activity level. This number is different for each person, but these are the average numbers:

- active men and teenage boys   → 2,800
- less active men, teenage girls, active women, and children   → 2,200
- less active women and older adults → 1,600

7   When you eat more calories than you need, your body will store most of the **excess** calories as fat. As a general rule for trimming off extra fat, you have to burn more calories over a period of time than you **consume.**

All Foods Are Not Equal

8   The calories in food come from three specific **nutrients:** fat, carbohydrates, and protein. Some foods contain only one or two of these three nutrients, but others contain all of them. In general, dairy products, nuts, fish, and meat contain calories that come mostly from fat and protein. Grains, fruits, and vegetables contain large amounts of carbohydrates. For example, chicken contains fat and protein, while blueberries contain mostly carbohydrates. Corn, however, contains all three.

9   What's important to realize is that fat, carbohydrates, and protein have different amounts of calories per gram:

- fat   ⟶   9 calories
- carbohydrates ⟶ 4 calories
- protein   ⟶ 4 calories

10   As you can see from the above list, a gram of fat contains more than twice as many calories as a gram of carbohydrates or protein. Why does this matter?

Add It Up

11   You calculate the number of calories in food by looking at the amounts of fat, carbohydrates, and protein it contains. Let's try this with low-fat milk, which has 2.5 grams of fat, 13 grams of carbohydrates, and 8 grams of protein per cup. The fat contains 23 calories (2.5 x 9), the carbohydrates contain 52 calories (13 x 4), and the protein contains 32 calories (8 x 4). When you add these together, you get a total of 107 calories (23 + 52 + 32).

1% Lowfat Milk   Grade A Pasteurized • Homogenized

Nutrition Facts	Amount/Serving	%DV*	Amount/Serving	%DV*
	Total Fat 2.5g	4%	Potassium 400mg	12%
Serving Size 1 cup (236mL)	Sat Fat 1.5g	8%	Total Carb. 13g	4%
	Trans Fat 0g		Dietary Fiber 0g	0%
Servings 16	Cholest. 15mg	4%	Sugars 13g	
Calories 107	Sodium 125mg	5%	Protein 8g	17%
Fat Cal. 20	Vitamin A 10% • Vitamin C 2% • Calcium 30%			
*Percent Daily Values (DV) are based on a 2,000 calorie diet.	Iron 0% • Vitamin D 25%			

Look at the types of calories in low-fat milk. Then look at the vitamins and minerals in the milk. **Think about whether or not low-fat milk is a healthy food choice.**

My WORKSPACE

Predict

Reread **paragraph 9**. Use this information to make a prediction. What else will the author say about fat, carbohydrates, and protein? Write your prediction on the lines below.

_____

_____

_____

_____

What clues from the text helped you make your prediction?

_____

_____

_____

_____

7

Predict

Review the "Put It to Work" section. Then look back at the prediction you wrote on page 7. Does your prediction match the information in the text? Why or why not?

_____

_____

_____

_____

_____

A turkey sandwich on whole-grain bread contains carbohydrates, protein, and fat. It also has vitamins and minerals. **Think about which parts of the sandwich have the most calories from fat, protein, and carbohydrates.**

8

12   Although you can calculate calories this way, you usually don't need to; the number of calories in packaged food is almost always listed on the label. For example, a label may tell you that a tablespoon of ketchup has 15 calories, a small granola bar has 100 calories, and a medium-size brownie has 243 calories.

13   Fat, carbohydrates, and protein also have specific jobs. Let's see how your body breaks down and uses these nutrients.

Put It to Work

14   Before your body can use food calories, it has to digest the food. As the food you eat passes through your stomach and intestines, **enzymes** break it down into new substances. Carbohydrates and fat are broken down into different kinds of sugar, which is used by your cells to make energy. Carbohydrates provide the majority of the energy your body uses to fuel organ functions and muscle movement. After your body runs out of carbohydrates, it uses its stored fat for energy. But the fat you eat helps your body absorb vitamins and minerals and plays an important part in many body functions.

15   The protein in your food is broken down into **amino acids.** Amino acids help build and maintain tissues in hair, skin, bones, and muscles. Protein calories aren't usually burned for energy. Your body will start to **convert** protein into energy only if it exhausts all other energy sources.

16   You can choose the types of calories you eat to match your physical goals. For example, if you were on the soccer team and had a game tomorrow, tonight you might want to eat a dinner that contains a lot of carbohydrates, such as pasta and vegetables. This would give you more available energy during your game. Another good reason to pay attention to the types of calories you eat is your overall health.

enzymes (en'-zīmz') the substances found in all living things that help chemical reactions, such as digestion of food, to take place
amino acids (ə-mē'-nō-a'-səds) the chemical substances that link together in long chains to form proteins in living things

Calories by Amount and Source

Food	Calories	Main Source
french fries medium order	380	fat, carbohydrates
chicken breast 4 oz., grilled	180	protein, fat
black beans 1 cup	227	carbohydrates, protein
spaghetti 1 cup	197	carbohydrates
apple 1 medium	80	carbohydrates
carrot 1 medium raw	35	carbohydrates

Think about how you could use this chart to choose a healthy snack.

Choose Wisely

17   Where do vitamins, minerals, and water fit into the calorie equation? They don't, because they don't contain any calories and don't provide any energy. However, they're essential to your health because they do specific jobs that help your cells work properly.

18   So what happens when you eat and drink foods such as potato chips, candy bars, or soda? All of these foods are high in calories because they contain a lot of fat or sugar, but they contain very few vitamins and minerals. For this reason, the calories in these foods are sometimes called "empty calories." These types of foods won't cause much harm if they are eaten in small amounts. If they are eaten regularly, however, they can lead to excess weight gain and poor nutrition.

19   So the next time you reach for a snack, consider passing up the chips and choosing low-fat cheese and vegetable sticks or a piece of fruit instead. By making wise choices, you can get the number of calories you need to keep your body healthy and maintain a good balance of nutrients too.

Self-Check
Look back at the prediction you wrote on page 3.
• Does your prediction match the text? Why or why not?

Now look back at the question you wrote on page 4.
• Does the information in the text answer your question? If it does, what is the answer? If it does not, where could you look to find more information?
Write your answers on a separate sheet of paper.

Understanding What You Read

Fill in the circle next to the correct answer. You may look back at the text to help you choose the correct answers.

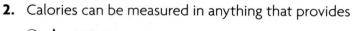

1. Gasoline is similar to fruit because they are both
   - ○ A. forms of protein.
   - ○ B. types of minerals.
   - ○ C. sources of energy.

2. Calories can be measured in anything that provides
   - ○ A. energy.
   - ○ B. food.
   - ○ C. heat.

3. If you could rename the "How Much Is Enough?" section, which of these would be the **best** choice?
   - ○ A. How Calories Affect Your Health
   - ○ B. The Calories You Need to Digest Food
   - ○ C. How Many Calories You Burn Every Day

4. From what the author told you about calories, you can conclude that
   - ○ A. your body is affected by both the amount and the type of calories you eat.
   - ○ B. the best way to give your body more nutrients is to eat more calories.
   - ○ C. people who exercise a lot need to eat mostly protein and fat.

5. The chart titled "Calories by Amount and Source" helps support the author's point that
   - ○ A. active men and teenage boys burn many calories.
   - ○ B. fruits and vegetables contain mostly carbohydrates.
   - ○ C. vitamins and minerals don't contain calories or provide energy.

Score 4 points for each correct answer.

_____/20 **Total Score: Activity A**

Making Predictions

Paragraph 2 from the article is shown below. Read the paragraph. Then use the paragraph to complete the activities.

> Of course, your body doesn't get its energy from gasoline; it gets energy from the food you eat. Different foods provide different amounts of energy. This energy is measured in calories.

1. Fill in the circle next to the prediction that is **best** supported by the above paragraph.
   - ○ A. I predict the author will explain how to measure the calories in food.
   - ○ B. I predict the author will explain what to do if you don't have enough energy.
   - ○ C. I predict the author will explain how much energy is in gasoline.

2. What clues from the text helped you choose the best prediction? How did what you already know help you choose the best prediction? Write your answers below.

   Clue _____

   Clue _____

   What I Know _____

   _____

   _____

Score 5 points each for numbers 1 and 2.

_____ /10   **Total Score: Activity B**

Using Words

Complete each sentence with a word from the box. Write the missing word on the line.

gender	excess	consume
nutrients	convert	

1. Vegetables are a healthy food choice because they contain important

   _____ .

2. My neighbor put an engine on his bicycle to _____ it into a motorcycle.

3. My cousin can _____ more food than I can because he is so much bigger than me.

4. My new puppy's _____ is female.

5. After knitting a sweater, she used the _____ yarn to make a hat.

Choose one word from the box. Write a new sentence using the word. Be sure to put at least one detail in your sentence. The detail should show that you understand what the word means. Use the sentences above as examples.

6. _____

   _____

Score 4 points for each correct answer in numbers 1–5.
(Do not score number 6.)

_____ /20   **Total Score: Activity C**

Writing About It

Write a Magazine Article Suppose you are a reporter for a health magazine. Write an article about food and calories. Finish the sentences below to write your article. Be sure your writing matches the information in the text. Use the checklist on page 119 to check your work.

Some people might associate calories only with gaining or losing weight. But there's more to calories than that, because _____

_____

_____

The three nutrients that provide calories are _____

_____

These nutrients are not equal when you are counting calories, because _____

_____

_____

Some high-calorie foods are unhealthy because _____

_____

_____

One way to eat healthier is to _____

_____

_____

_____

Lesson 1 Add your scores from activities A, B, and C to get your total score.

_____ **A** Understanding What You Read
_____ **B** Making Predictions
_____ **C** Using Words
_____ **Total Score**

Multiply your **Total Score x 2** _____
This is your percentage score.
Record your percentage score on the graph on page 121.

POPCORN
Snack Time

Popcorn is a popular snack that comes with an interesting story.

READING SKILL **Making Connections**

Good readers **make connections** as they read. They use what they already know and their own life experience to connect to the text. Making connections helps you stay interested in what you are reading. It can also help you understand the text on a deeper or more personal level. To make connections, think about what the text reminds you of. Think also about how your connection helps you better understand the text.

EXAMPLE

Popcorn first became very popular around the 1890s. This was a time when popcorn vendors used rolling street carts to make and sell their popcorn. Popcorn was sold at parades, carnivals, and sporting events. People could buy a bag of popcorn for only a nickel.

Look at these examples of strong and weak connections for the example paragraph above.

Weak Connection

The text reminds me of the last time I ate popcorn.

Strong Connection

When I read about popcorn being sold at sporting events, it reminds me of the baseball game I went to last weekend because my brother and I shared a bag of popcorn there.

Complete the sentences below to make a strong connection to the information in the example paragraph.

When I read about _____

it reminds me _____

_____

because _____

_____

This helps me understand _____

_____

Getting Ready to Read

Think About What You Know

CONNECT Think about the last time you watched, heard, or smelled popcorn popping. Where were you? What are all the different ways you know of to make popcorn? Write your answers here.

_____

_____

_____

Word Power

PREVIEW Read the words and definitions below. Then look ahead at the title and at the headings and images in the article.

consists (kən-sists′)	is formed
distributed (di-stri′-būt-əd)	spread over an area
ruptures (rəp′-shərz)	breaks open
fuse (fūz)	to join separate things together so that they become one thing
sufficient (sə-fi′-shənt)	as much as needed to suit a specific purpose

PREDICT Use the words, title, headings, and images to make a prediction. What do you think the author will say about popcorn?

I predict the author will _____

_____

because _____

_____

Reason to Read

Read to find out if the prediction you wrote above matches the information in the text. At the end of the article, you will be asked about your prediction. You will need to explain how your prediction is the same as the text or different from it.

POPCORN Snack Time

Popcorn looks like most other types of corn when it's still on the cob. **Think about how people might have discovered popcorn.**

1   It's happened to every popcorn lover. You curl up on the couch with a bowl of popcorn to watch a movie. You're happily tossing popcorn into your mouth when suddenly you bite down on something hard: a kernel that didn't pop.

2   Why didn't this little kernel pop like the rest of them? Let's look at what makes popcorn pop to find the answer.

Corn Basics

3   Thousands of years ago people discovered that hard kernels of corn would pop open when heated, allowing people to eat them. In fact, many experts believe that popcorn was the original type of corn. Today there are many types of corn, and popcorn is one of the most common. Other types include sweet corn, which is the kind you can eat on the cob; field corn, which people use as cattle feed and to make food products such as corn oil; and flint corn, which people use to produce cornmeal.

4   Corn is a cereal grain, like wheat or oats, so it has an inner core and an outer shell as all such grains do. The core of a popcorn kernel **consists** mostly of starch, which is a form of **carbohydrate.** The core also contains protein, fat, minerals, and a small amount of water. This moisture, which is **distributed** evenly throughout the core, plays an important role in making the kernel pop.

5   A hard outer shell surrounds the core of the kernel. On most other grains the shell is soft, but on popcorn it's very hard. If you've ever bitten into a kernel that hasn't popped, you know just how hard this shell is! The hard shell also plays an important role in making popcorn pop.

carbohydrate (kär'-bō-hī'-drāt') one of the chemical compounds found in food

Predict

Reread the shaded text in **paragraphs 4** and **5.** Use this information to make a prediction. What will the author say about what makes popcorn pop?

_____

_____

_____

_____

_____

What clues from the text helped you make your prediction?

_____

_____

_____

_____

Connect

Use the information in the shaded text to make a connection. Complete the sentence below.

When I read about moisture turning to steam, it reminds me

_____

_____

_____

because _____

_____

_____

_____

Predict

When you've finished reading this page, look back at the prediction you wrote on page 17. Does your prediction match the information in the text? Why or why not?

_____

_____

_____

_____

The *Pop* in Popcorn

6   You've probably seen what happens when you put a pot of water on a hot stove: the water starts to bubble, and then it turns to steam. A similar thing happens when a kernel of popcorn is heated: the moisture in the core turns to steam. When water gets hot and turns to steam, water **molecules** move away from each other and take up more and more space. This is why the hard outer shell is so important. If the kernel's outer shell were soft, the steam would easily leak out of the core. However, because the shell is hard, it contains the steam— at least for a while.

7   With the shell holding firm, pressure builds inside the kernel. When the temperature of the steam reaches 400°F to 450°F (204°C to 232°C), the pressure becomes so intense that it **ruptures** the kernel's shell. This happens with a sudden *pop!*

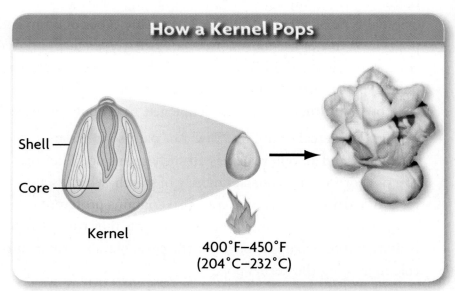

How a Kernel Pops

Shell

Core

Kernel

400°F–450°F
(204°C–232°C)

This diagram shows a kernel before and after it pops. Look at the labeled kernel on the left. Then look at the the popped kernel on the right. The core of the popped kernel has expanded and the shell has broken into pieces. Can you see the pieces of the shell in the popped kernel? **Think about how the positions of the shell and the core change when the kernel pops.**

molecules (mä′-li-kūlz′) the smallest complete particles of a substance

8   As the shell breaks, the soft starch in the core expands and bursts out, creating many tiny bubbles. These bubbles **fuse** together and rapidly cool, forming the fluffy, familiar shape we know as popcorn. One piece of perfectly popped popcorn can be as much as 40 times larger than its kernel!

Duds

9   What about that annoying unpopped kernel? There could be a couple of reasons why it failed to pop. One possibility is that the kernel's outer shell was cracked, which would have allowed steam to leak out before it created enough pressure to rupture the shell.

10   The other possibility is that there wasn't **sufficient** moisture inside that particular kernel. Popcorn pops best when the core is between 13 and 14 percent moisture. If there isn't enough moisture, there won't be enough steam pressure to make the kernel pop. If there is too much moisture, the core will rupture before the starch inside gets hot enough to fully expand, leaving you with a small, hard, half-popped kernel.

From Field to Store

11   Because the amount of moisture in a kernel is critical to its ability to pop, it's important to harvest, or pick, the ears of popcorn at just the right time. Farmers know it's best to let the corn stand in the field and dry naturally, but if they wait too long, the cornstalks might topple over or become damaged by rain. Ideally, popcorn is picked when the moisture content is about 16 percent. Farmers know the time is right when the plant's leaves and stalk have become brown and dry, and a thin, black layer of cells has formed at the base of the kernels.

Connect

Use the information in **paragraph 10** to make a connection. Complete the sentence below.

When I read about _____

_____

_____

it reminds me _____

_____

_____

because _____

_____

_____

_____

Using a combine to pick popcorn saves a lot of time. **Think about how much longer it would take to pick the corn and separate the kernels without this machine.**

12   Farmers typically pick popcorn with a machine called a combine, which separates the cob from the stalk and removes the kernels from the cob. Then farmers take the kernels to a place for processing. There the kernels go into a bin where air, circulating through vents in the bottom, dries them. When they reach the proper moisture level, the kernels are placed on vibrating screens that shake out debris. After they've been cleaned and polished, the kernels are packaged for sale.

Is It Healthy?

13   Popcorn has several great qualities, including the fact that it's a whole-grain food and therefore an excellent source of energy-providing carbohydrates. But popcorn's status as a healthy food can change depending on how you prepare it.

14   Plain popcorn prepared in an air popper is low in calories and a good source of fiber. It also has no sugar and no **preservatives.** But adding oil, butter, or cheese powder can turn popcorn into junk food because these ingredients add large quantities of fat. Some types of microwave and movie popcorn contain more fat calories per serving than many nutrition experts recommend. Heavily salted popcorn can also be unhealthy. So it's important to pay attention to how popcorn is prepared.

Popcorn Caution

15   Here are a few other tips about popcorn. First, eat it carefully. If you chomp down on a kernel that didn't pop properly, you could chip a tooth or lose a filling. Also, do not give very young children popcorn; it could get caught in their tiny throats. And finally, it's a good idea to use dental floss after eating popcorn because bits of popcorn often get stuck between teeth and in gums.

preservatives (pri-zər'-və-tivz) the chemicals that are added to foods to keep them from spoiling quickly

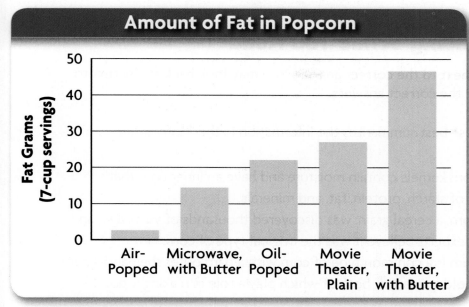

Amount of Fat in Popcorn

Fat Grams
(7-cup servings)

50
40
30
20
10
0

Air-Popped | Microwave, with Butter | Oil-Popped | Movie Theater, Plain | Movie Theater, with Butter

This bar graph compares the fat content in five different types of popcorn. Experts recommend that people eat 65 to 70 fat grams or less per day. **Think about how the amount of fat shown for each type of popcorn compares to the recommended daily amount.**

16   But those few stubborn kernels and that extra time spent on dental care haven't scared off popcorn lovers. Each year people in the United States eat more than 17 billion quarts of popcorn. Imagine a large laundry basket filled to the brim with popcorn, and you'll get a sense of how much popcorn each person eats per year.

17   The pressure of all this popularity might be too much for other snack foods, but for popcorn, dealing with pressure is what it's all about.

Did You Know?
- In 2003 the state of Illinois declared popcorn its official snack food.
- More popcorn is sold during scary movies than other kinds of movies.
- During the 1920s, popcorn was banned in many movie theaters because eating it was considered too noisy.

Self-Check
Look back at the prediction you wrote on page 16.
- Does your prediction match the text? Why or why not?

Write your answers on a separate sheet of paper.

Understanding What You Read

Fill in the circle next to the correct answer. You may look back at the text to help you choose the correct answers.

1. Which of these **best** summarizes the information in the "Corn Basics" section?
    - ○ A. Popcorn kernels contain moisture and have an inner core that's made of starch, protein, fat, and minerals.
    - ○ B. Popcorn, a cereal grain, was discovered thousands of years ago, and many experts believe it was the original type of corn.
    - ○ C. Popcorn is a common type of corn with a hard outer shell and a core that holds moisture, both of which play a role in making it pop.

2. Popcorn is different from many other cereal grains because
    - ○ A. it has an inner core.
    - ○ B. its outer shell is hard.
    - ○ C. the kernel holds moisture.

3. The amount of moisture in a kernel
    - ○ A. is critical to its ability to pop.
    - ○ B. increases as the corn gets older.
    - ○ C. stays between 13 and 14 percent.

4. The bar graph titled "Amount of Fat in Popcorn" helps support the author's point that
    - ○ A. it's important to pay attention to how popcorn is prepared.
    - ○ B. popcorn is a good snack because it's a whole-grain food.
    - ○ C. adding too much salt to popcorn makes it unhealthy.

5. The author included the information in the "Did You Know?" box on page 21 in order to
    - ○ A. express his or her opinion about popcorn.
    - ○ B. restate several main ideas from the article.
    - ○ C. increase the reader's enjoyment of the article.

Score 4 points for each correct answer.

_____ /20   **Total Score: Activity A**

Making Connections

Two paragraphs from the article are shown below. Read each paragraph. Then use each paragraph to complete the activity that follows it.

As the shell breaks, the soft starch in the core expands and bursts out, creating many tiny bubbles. These bubbles fuse together and rapidly cool, forming the fluffy, familiar shape we know as popcorn. One piece of perfectly popped popcorn can be as much as 40 times larger than its kernel!

1. Complete the sentence to make a strong connection to the paragraph above.

When I read about _____

it reminds me _____

_____

because _____

_____

Farmers typically pick popcorn with a machine called a combine, which separates the cob from the stalk and removes the kernels from the cob. Then farmers take the kernels to a place for processing. There the kernels go into a bin where air, circulating through vents in the bottom, dries them. When they reach the proper moisture level, the kernels are placed on vibrating screens that shake out debris. After they've been cleaned and polished, the kernels are packaged for sale.

2. Use what you already know to make a strong connection to the information in the paragraph above. Write your connection below.

_____

_____

_____

_____

Score 5 points each for numbers 1 and 2.

_____ /10   **Total Score: Activity B**

Using Words

Follow the instructions below. Write your answers on the lines.

1. List **two** qualities of something that **consists** of glass.

    _____

    _____

2. List **three** things that might be **distributed** in a school lunchroom.

    _____

    _____

    _____

3. List **two** things that happen when a balloon **ruptures.**

    _____

    _____

4. List **two** sets of things that can **fuse** together.

    _____

    _____

5. List **two** ways you can tell that someone has had **sufficient** sleep.

    _____

    _____

Score 4 points for each correct answer.

_____ /20   **Total Score: Activity C**

Writing About It

Write an Advertisement Suppose you work for a company that sells popcorn. Write an advertisement that will make people want to buy your company's popcorn. Finish the sentences below to write your advertisement. Be sure your writing matches the information in the text. Use the checklist on page 119 to check your work.

Zippy-Pop Popcorn
is delicious!

People love Zippy-Pop Popcorn because _____

_____

_____

With Zippy-Pop Popcorn, you won't have a lot of unpopped

kernels because _____

_____

You will be amazed by _____

_____

Zippy-Pop Popcorn is good for you because _____

_____

Try Zippy-Pop Popcorn tonight!

Lesson 2 Add your scores from activities A, B, and C to get your total score.

_____ **A** Understanding What You Read
_____ **B** Making Connections
_____ **C** Using Words
_____ **Total Score**   Multiply your **Total Score x 2** _____
                                    This is your percentage score.
                        Record your percentage score on the graph on page 121.

GENETICALLY MODIFIED FOOD
BOOM OR DOOM?

Some people think genetically (jə-ne′-ti-klē) modified foods provide great benefits, but others worry about how they might affect us in the future.

READING SKILL **Visualizing**

Good readers create pictures in their minds as they read. They use details from the text to **visualize** what the author is describing. Authors may include details about color, shape, size, and movement. Details may also help you visualize relationships and how things work. The mental pictures that you create come from what you already know and from your imagination. Creating pictures in your mind will help you understand the text. It will also help you remember more of what you read.

EXAMPLE

Believe it or not, some weeds can be very helpful to farmers. The roots of helpful weeds help hold soil in place when there are heavy rains or strong winds. The flowers of helpful weeds draw harmful insects away from crops. One example of a good weed is the milkweed plant. Milkweed plants have long stems, large green leaves, and clusters of pink flowers.

The details in the example paragraph above can help you visualize what some helpful weeds look like and how they help farmers. Think about the detail words *roots, hold soil, heavy rains, strong winds, draw harmful insects away, long stems, large green leaves,* and *clusters of pink flowers.* Then think about what a garden or a farm looks like. Use your imagination and what you already know to help you visualize these helpful weeds in a garden or on a farm.

Draw a picture of what you are visualizing in the box below. Include as many details as possible in your drawing.

Getting Ready to Read

Think About What You Know

CONNECT Think about the foods you eat on a regular basis. What do you know about where your food comes from and how it is grown? Write your answers here.

_____

_____

_____

Word Power

PREVIEW Read the words and definitions below. Then look ahead at the title and at the headings and images in the article.

controversial (kän'-trə-vər'-shəl)	causing many arguments due to strong opinions about the topic
characteristics (kar'-ik-tə-ris'-tiks)	the qualities or features of something that are common to it and that set it apart from other things
tolerate (tä'-lə-rāt')	to put up with or allow something even though you don't like it
disrupts (dis-rəpts')	keeps something from continuing its normal activities or its desired path by creating a problem
ineffective (i'-nə-fek'-tiv)	not able to produce the desired results

QUESTION Use the words, title, headings, and images to ask a question. What would you like to know about genetically modified food? Write your question on the lines below.

_____

_____

_____

Reason to Read

Read to find out if the information in the text answers your question. At the end of the article, you will be asked to look back at your question. You will decide whether or not your question is answered in the text.

GENETICALLY MODIFIED FOOD
BOOM OR DOOM?

1   Do you ever think about where your food comes from? Have you ever heard of genetically modified food? Get ready to read about a new and **controversial** way of growing food.

How Genes Work

2   Genetically modified (GM) food is food that comes from plants with genetic codes that have been directly changed by humans. The word *genetic* refers to the genes of living things, which are passed from one generation to the next. Genes are found in the center of almost every living cell. The tiny genes carry detailed instructions for how a living thing will look, move, and grow. In humans, genes determine everything from eye color to foot size. In plants, genes determine how much water and sun a plant needs, how it reacts to disease, and so on.

3   What does this have to do with food? Well, scientists have found a way to mix the genes in different living things. By inserting genes for certain **characteristics** into a plant, scientists can change the way a plant naturally grows. How does this work?

In the Laboratory

4   Living things have thousands of genes. The genes are found within **molecules** of DNA, or deoxyribonucleic acid. A DNA molecule has a spiral shape called a double helix, which looks a bit like a twisted ladder. Genes are found all along the DNA molecules, which coil up to form structures called chromosomes. A chromosome looks like the letter *X*.

---

molecules (mä'-li-kūlz') the smallest complete particles of a substance

Visualize

Reread the shaded text. Write **two** details from the text that help you visualize the qualities in humans and plants that are determined by genes.

1. _____
   _____

2. _____
   _____

Use the details in the text and what you already know to visualize what the author is describing. Draw what you are visualizing in the box below.

Reread **paragraphs 5** and **6**. Write **two** details from the text that help you visualize scientists creating the genetic map of a rice plant.

1. _____

   _____

2. _____

   _____

Use the details in the text and what you already know to visualize scientists creating a genetic map. Draw what you are visualizing in the box below.

Genes, Chromosomes, and DNA

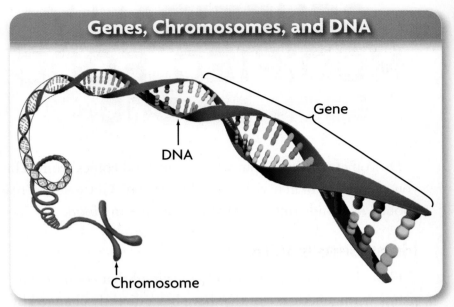

This diagram shows how the DNA molecule coils into a chromosome. Each gene is actually a section of the DNA molecule. There are hundreds of genes in each chromosome. The number of chromosomes in living things varies. Humans have 46 chromosomes in each cell. **Think about how tiny and complex genes are.**

5   Genes help determine the specific characteristics of an **organism,** such as its leaf size or need for water. Scientists study each complex gene very closely to figure out which genes correspond to which characteristic. This allows them to create a map that shows the location of each gene on a chromosome and what that gene does.

6   Creating a genetic map is a long and expensive process. It took six years for an international group of scientists to map out the genes of a rice plant. But once a genetic map is complete, the genes of an organism can be modified in a single day using special laboratory techniques that change DNA molecules. Why would scientists go through all this trouble?

---

organism (ôr′-gə-ni′-zəm) any living thing, such as a plant or an animal

Genes and Food

7   Growing crops that produce large amounts of food can be challenging. For one thing, farmers have to protect crops from pests such as insects and rodents that can eat entire plants and leave little to harvest. Many farmers use chemical **pesticides** to protect their crops, but these are expensive and can harm the environment.

8   Also, it can be very difficult to grow food in areas affected by extreme weather. Heavy rains, flooding, or drought can destroy crops. By modifying genes, scientists hope to give plants characteristics that allow them to survive in harsh conditions.

New Kinds of Plants

9   In nature genes pass only between parents and offspring. However, genetic modification allows scientists to cross genes between organisms that aren't related at all. This can result in dramatic changes in a plant. For example, scientists identified a **bacterium** in soil that makes certain insects sick. By putting genes from this bacterium into a corn plant, scientists produced corn plants that poison the insects that feed on them. When a plant can kill insects on its own, the farmer doesn't have to spray as much pesticide on the crop. This saves money and helps protect the environment.

10   Genetic modification can affect plants in other ways too. It can make plants better able to fight disease, or it can allow them to produce more vitamins. Plants have also been modified to **tolerate** poisons in weed killers, making it possible to spray an entire field and kill only the weeds.

11   In places where food is scarce, these changes could make a big difference. GM rice in Asia is one example of this.

---

pesticides (pes'-tə-sīdz') the chemicals that are dropped or sprayed on crops to kill insects or small animals that feed on the crops
bacterium (bak-tir'-ē-əm) a very tiny living thing made of only one cell; some live inside healthy animals and some can cause diseases

Visualize

What details in the shaded text might help you visualize the damage pests can do to crops? Write **two** details below.

1. _____

   _____

2. _____

   _____

What would you have to already know to be able to use these details to visualize?

_____

_____

_____

_____

_____

GM crops, like this GM corn crop, look like regular crops. **Think about whether or not you would be able to recognize GM corn in the grocery store.**

Common GM Foods			
GM Food	New Characteristic	Source of Gene	Purpose
corn, cotton	resists insects	disease-causing bacterium	to reduce insect damage and the use of pesticides
soybeans, canola	is not harmed by poisons in weed killers	soil bacterium	to aid weed control

The largest GM crops in the United States include soybeans, corn, canola, and cotton. This chart shows how and why each crop is modified. **Think about how these four GM crops are similar.**

GM Rice in Asia

12   Rice is the primary food crop in Asia, where millions of people don't have enough to eat. In an effort to increase the supply of food, scientists created GM rice. As with corn, they modified the rice to be poisonous to insects. Farmers were then able to reduce their use of pesticides by 80 percent and to harvest 10 percent more of the grain.

13   Scientists also have been experimenting with increasing the amount of vitamin A available from rice by adding genes from two types of daffodil flowers and a gene from a bacterium. Sadly, 250,000 to 500,000 children in the world go blind each year from the lack of vitamin A. There is hope that creating this new rice will help prevent blindness in millions of children.

14   Sounds like a happy ending, right? Not so fast. Despite these benefits, there's a great deal of controversy about GM foods.

Unknown Effects

15   Some people believe that genetic modification crosses a dangerous line because it **disrupts** the very foundation of life: genetic codes. They point out that there's no way to know the long-term effects GM crops might have on the environment— and on people.

Predict

Reread **paragraph 15.** Use this information and what you already know to make a prediction. What will the author say about how genetic modification might cause problems?

_____

_____

_____

_____

How did the clues in the text and what you already know help you make your prediction?

_____

_____

_____

_____

_____

16   For instance, plant pollen travels on the wind and is also carried from plant to plant by insects. How can farmers prevent the pollen of GM crops from mixing with the pollen of regular crops? And what if pollen from poison-tolerant GM crops mixes with weeds? The weeds could become "super weeds" that tolerate chemical poisons. In fact, Canada has already reported problems with GM canola plants themselves becoming super weeds. Farmers can't keep the GM canola plants from spreading among their other crops—and they can't kill them.

17   And what about helpful insects such as monarch butterflies, which feed off plants that grow near cornfields? Could poisonous GM corn pollen kill off these beautiful animals?

18   It's also unclear whether GM foods might pose a health risk to the animals and people who eat them. There is concern that people may become allergic to the unfamiliar genes in some GM foods. Some say that these genes could get into the bacteria that live inside the human body, causing lifesaving medicines such as antibiotics to become **ineffective.** Could GM foods cause other unforeseen changes in humans? We simply don't know.

19   Is it worth the risk? Many people say no, especially in Europe, where laws have been passed against some GM foods. But many people in the United States point to the benefits.

GM Food in the United States

20   Today more than 60 percent of all **processed foods** in the United States contain some GM ingredients. U.S. laws do not require food labels to include information about genetically modified ingredients. So chances are you've been eating GM foods whether you know it or not.

22   But whether we like them or not, GM foods are already a part of our lives. And the controversy surrounding them is likely to continue for years to come.

---

processed foods (prä′-sest-fōōdz′) foods that have had things added to them or that have been changed in some way so that they last longer or taste better

TOMATO PUREE

MADE WITH **GENETICALLY MODIFIED TOMATOES**

This can of GM tomatoes is from Great Britain. **Think about why people would want labels on genetically modified foods.**

Predict
When you've finished reading this page, look back at the prediction you wrote on page 32. Does your prediction match the text? Why or why not?

_____

_____

_____

_____

Self-Check
Look back at the question you wrote on page 28.
• Does the information in the text answer your question? If it does, what is the answer? If it does not, where could you look to find more information?
Write your answers on a separate sheet of paper.

Understanding What You Read

Fill in the circle next to the correct answer. You may look back at the text to help you choose the correct answers.

1. Genes are found
   - ○ A. in water, sunshine, and seeds.
   - ○ B. only in crops such as soybeans.
   - ○ C. in the center of almost every living cell.

2. Which step has to happen **before** the genes in a plant can be modified?
   - ○ A. Scientists complete a genetic map.
   - ○ B. Farmers begin to grow stronger crops.
   - ○ C. Consumers decide that they want GM food.

3. What was one effect of putting an insect-killing bacterium gene in corn?
   - ○ A. GM crops mixed with regular crops.
   - ○ B. Corn began to provide more vitamins.
   - ○ C. Farmers were able to use fewer chemicals.

4. The chart titled "Common GM Foods" helps support the author's point that
   - ○ A. pollen from GM crops that tolerate poisons could mix with the pollen in weeds and turn them into super weeds.
   - ○ B. genetic modification allows scientists to cross genes between organisms that aren't related at all.
   - ○ C. scientists created GM rice in an effort to increase the supply of food in Asia.

5. From the information in the article, you can infer that
   - ○ A. most lawmakers in the United States think that GM products should be clearly labeled.
   - ○ B. certain kinds of snack chips made in the United States probably contain GM ingredients.
   - ○ C. food made in Europe is more likely to contain GM ingredients than food made in the United States.

Score 4 points for each correct answer.

_____ /20   **Total Score: Activity A**

Visualizing

Paragraph 16 from the article is shown below. Read the paragraph. Then use the paragraph to complete the activities.

> For instance, plant pollen travels on the wind and is also carried from plant to plant by insects. How can farmers prevent the pollen of GM crops from mixing with the pollen of regular crops? And what if pollen from poison-tolerant GM crops mixes with weeds? The weeds could become "super weeds" that tolerate chemical poisons. In fact, Canada has already reported problems with GM canola plants themselves becoming super weeds. Farmers can't keep the GM canola plants from spreading among their other crops—and they can't kill them.

1. Write **three** details from the paragraph that help you visualize how GM crops might affect other crops. Then write what you already know about wind that helps you visualize this.

    Detail _____

    Detail _____

    Detail _____

    What I Know _____

    _____

2. Use the details from the paragraph and what you already know to create a picture in your mind. Draw what you are visualizing in the box below.

Using Words

The words and phrases in the list below relate to the words in the box. Some words or phrases in the list are synonyms. They have the same meaning. Some words or phrases are antonyms. They have the opposite meaning. Write the related word from the box on each line. Use each word from the box **twice.**

controversial	characteristics	tolerate
disrupts	ineffective	

Synonyms

1. qualities _____

2. useless _____

3. upsets _____

4. features _____

5. accept _____

6. debatable _____

Antonyms

7. agreed-upon _____

8. supports _____

9. reject _____

10. helpful _____

Score 2 points for each correct answer.

_____ /20   **Total Score: Activity C**

Writing About It

Write a Speech Suppose you are asked to give a speech about genetically modified food. Write a speech that discusses both the positive and negative points about genetically modified food. Finish the sentences below to write your speech. Be sure your writing matches the information in the text. Use the checklist on page 119 to check your work.

Genetically modified food is food that comes from _____

_____

Plants are genetically modified in order to _____

_____

_____

Some people believe genetic modification is helpful because _____

_____

_____

Some people believe genetic modification is dangerous because _____

_____

_____

_____

From what I've read, I think _____

_____

_____

_____

Lesson 3 Add your scores from activities A, B, and C to get your total score.

_____ **A** Understanding What You Read

_____ **B** Visualizing

_____ **C** Using Words

_____ **Total Score**

Multiply your **Total Score x 2** _____

This is your percentage score.

Record your percentage score on the graph on page 121.

Compare and Contrast

You read three articles about food in Unit One. Think about the topic of each article. Then choose **two** of the articles. Write the titles of the articles in the Venn diagram below. In the left and right circles, write the differences between the ways these two topics affect people's lives. In the section where the two circles overlap, write the similarities in how they affect people's lives.

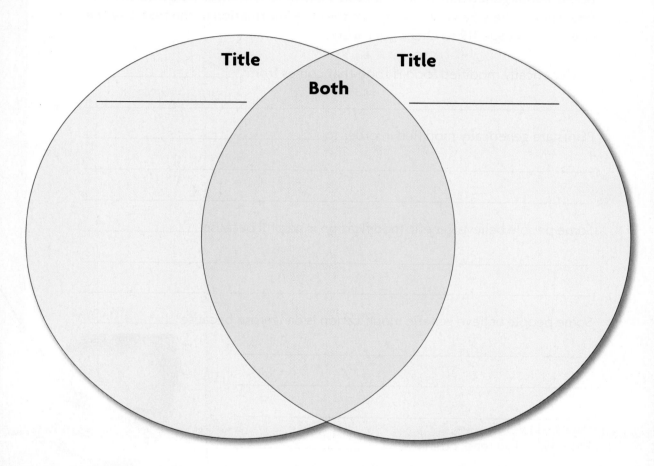

Title

Both

Title

_____

_____

Use the diagram above to write a summary of how these food topics are alike and different. Finish the sentences below to write your summary.

_____ and _____ are different

because _____

_____

_____ and _____ are similar

because _____

_____

Unit 2

Nature

Venus Flytraps

Mudslides

Mosquitoes

VENUS FLYTRAPS
Meat-Eating Plants

These Venus flytraps wait for an insect or a spider to provide a tasty meal.

READING SKILL **Asking Questions**

Good readers **ask questions** before, during, and after reading. Asking questions can help you set a purpose for reading. It can also help you stay interested in the text and find more meaning as you read. Sometimes your questions will be answered later in the text. At other times you will have to find the answers on your own. You could do this by asking your teacher or another student for help. You could also look for the answer on the Internet or in a book or magazine at the library.

EXAMPLE

When most people think of flower gardens, they think of sweet-smelling blossoms with bright and cheerful colors. Some gardeners, however, enjoy growing unusual plants. One such plant is the dragon arum. A long, slender black stalk grows upwards from its large, purplish flower. The flower releases a powerful scent that is similar to the smell of rotting meat.

What does the dragon arum plant look like? is a good question to ask yourself as you read the example paragraph above. This question is answered in the fourth sentence of the paragraph.

Why does the dragon arum plant have such a bad smell? is another good question you might ask. This question is **not** answered in the paragraph text. To find the answer, you would need to go beyond the text. On the lines below, describe one thing you could do to answer this question.

_____

_____

Now think about the article you are about to read. Use the image on the previous page and what you already know to ask a question about Venus flytraps. Write your question on the lines below.

_____

_____

Getting Ready to Read

Think About What You Know

CONNECT Think about animals that eat meat. How do they trap and eat their prey? What do you know about plants that eat meat? How might a plant trap and eat its prey? Write your answers here.

_____

_____

_____

Word Power

PREVIEW Read the words and definitions below. Then look ahead at the title and at the headings and images in the article.

predators (pre′-də-tərz)	animals that survive by hunting and killing other animals
intriguing (in-trē′-ging)	causing interest and curiosity
supplement (sə′-plə-mənt)	something that is added to make up for what is missing
edible (e′-də-bəl)	able to be eaten
vulnerable (vəl′-nə-rə-bəl)	capable of being attacked or hurt

PREDICT Use the words, title, headings, and images to make a prediction. What do you think the author will say about Venus flytraps?

I predict the author will _____

_____

because _____

_____

Reason to Read

Read to find out if the prediction you wrote above matches the information in the text. At the end of the article, you will be asked about your prediction. You will need to explain how your prediction is the same as the text or different from it.

VENUS FLYTRAPS
Meat-Eating Plants

1 The world can be a dangerous place for a fly. If it ventures inside a house, it may get whacked by a flyswatter. And outside, natural **predators** are a threat; frogs wait near ponds, and bats wait in trees.

2 Maybe a field of plants is a safe bet. That is, unless Venus flytraps grow there. If a fly lands on a Venus flytrap's leaf, that fly will be dinner in the blink of an eye.

One Hungry Plant

3 The Venus flytrap is one of more than 500 **species** of carnivorous, or meat-eating, plants. It is native to the coastal regions of North and South Carolina, where it thrives in damp, boggy areas. Because these plants are so **intriguing,** many people also grow them indoors as houseplants.

4 In many ways, there isn't anything particularly unique about a Venus flytrap; it stands about eight to 12 inches (20 to 30 cm) tall, and like so many other plants, it sprouts flowers. The thing that makes the Venus flytrap so fascinating is its traps. Each trap on the plant is made of a leaf that is hinged in the middle so it can fold shut, similar to the way a clam's shell does. When closed, an average trap is slightly larger than a quarter. Each trap has six short, stiff trigger hairs—three on the inside of each side of the leaf. In addition, thin and spiky extensions called cilia surround the trap's edges.

A Venus flytrap houseplant requires great care and special treatment. **Think about things people might have to do for a Venus flytrap that they wouldn't have to do for other houseplants.**

Predict

Reread the shaded text. Use this information to make a prediction. What will the author say about how Venus flytraps catch flies? Write your prediction on the lines below.

_____

_____

_____

_____

What clues from the text helped you make your prediction?

_____

_____

_____

_____

species (spē'-shēz) a particular variety of plant or animal life

43

5   But if a Venus flytrap is a plant, why does it eat meat? After all, plants create their own food through photosynthesis, a process that uses sunlight to turn carbon dioxide and water into sugar. They can also get some nutrients from the soil. The Venus flytrap is capable of getting nutrients in these ways too. But because the boggy soil where it grows doesn't have enough nutrients, it eats insects and other bugs as a **supplement.**

Snap!

6   Because the Venus flytrap can't go to the bug, it makes the bug come to it. The plant releases a sweet-smelling **nectar** into the trap. This nectar and the red color of the inside of the leaf lure crickets, spiders, and other bugs into the trap.

7   When the bug crawls around in the trap, it touches the trap's trigger hairs. If the bug touches two triggers (or the same trigger twice), the two halves of the trap's leaf snap shut with amazing speed. As a matter of fact, the trap snaps shut in one-tenth of a second! Have you ever tried to swat a fly? It was gone before your hand got anywhere near it, right? That should help you understand just how quickly the leaf needs to shut to catch that fly.

8   Sometimes a twig or pebble falls into the trap, bending only a single hair one time. If there's only one touch, the trap senses that whatever is in it isn't alive. Because it's not worthwhile for it to close unless there's live food in it, the trap won't shut.

Predict

Reread the shaded text. Then look back at the prediction you wrote on page 43. Does your prediction match the text? Why or why not?

_____

_____

_____

_____

nectar (nek'-tər) a sweet liquid produced by some plants

Parts of the Venus Flytrap

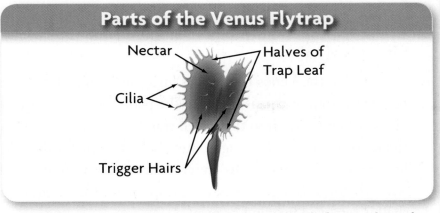

Nectar

Halves of Trap Leaf

Cilia

Trigger Hairs

Think about why the trigger hairs are spread out instead of grouped together.

9   What exactly causes the halves of the leaf to shut continues to be a mystery. Humans can react quickly to things because we have nerves and muscles that respond instantly to what's around us. But a Venus flytrap has neither nerves nor muscles. This fact is at the root of the mystery surrounding the plant's ability to respond so quickly.

10   Recent research has shown that the shape of the trap's leaf is the key to the snapping action. When they are open, the halves of the trap's leaf are curved outwards. After something touches the triggers, fluid in the plant is pumped into the leaf. This fluid puts pressure on the halves, causing them to bend inwards. When the halves of the leaf cannot resist the pressure any longer, they snap shut.

Seal the Deal

11   When the trap closes, it doesn't seal completely shut right away. But the cilia do lock together to keep some prey from escaping. Take a moment to lace the fingers of your hands together, and you can see how this works.

12   Because the trap doesn't seal shut immediately, smaller bugs can still crawl out. Digesting prey requires energy, and it's not worthwhile for the plant to spend energy to digest prey unless the prey will provide plenty of energy in return. Larger bugs provide more energy, so the plant makes sure they can't get out. As they thrash around and try to escape, they touch the trigger hairs again, causing the leaf to close entirely. Within just a few minutes, the halves of the leaf form an airtight seal.

Ask Questions

Reread **paragraph 9**. What question would you like to ask about the information in this paragraph? Write your question on the lines below.

_____

_____

_____

How does asking this question help you stay engaged in the text as you read?

_____

_____

_____

The sticky hairs of the sundew, another carnivorous plant, easily trap bugs that land on them. **Think about why a bug might be drawn to a sundew.**

46

Soup's On!

13   Now that the Venus flytrap has lured and trapped its prey, it begins to work on its tasty meal. The plant "eats" by releasing digestive **enzymes** into the sealed trap to dissolve the soft inner tissues of the bug. The tough outer shell of an insect doesn't have many nutrients, so the enzymes aren't meant to dissolve it. After the meal is digested and the trap opens, the insect's empty shell is removed by wind or rain.

14   It takes the Venus flytrap five to 12 days to completely digest a bug. The actual time depends on several factors, such as the size of the bug, the age of the trap, and the temperature of the air.

Not Quite Perfect

15   As efficient as the Venus flytrap's system is, it can still run into problems. Sometimes the trap does close around an object that isn't **edible,** such as a pebble or twig. After about 12 hours, the trap reopens, releasing the unwanted object. But for a plant that can use each trap only a limited number of times, this is a costly mistake. Each false alarm brings the trap closer to the end of its trapping abilities. When a trap retires from catching insects, it stays open and helps the plant with photosynthesis.

---

enzymes (en′-zīmz′) the substances found in all living things that help chemical reactions, such as digestion of food, to take place

After the trap seals shut, the plant releases digestive substances into it to "eat" its prey. **Think about what types of creatures Venus flytraps might "eat."**

16   Sometimes the Venus flytrap bites off more than it can chew. If a trap closes around prey that's bigger than itself, part of the bug will be left dangling outside of it. The plant's digestive enzymes will still go to work inside the trap, but the plant cannot form the seal around the bug's body. This makes the trap **vulnerable** to **bacteria** that eat the bug, eventually causing the trap itself to rot.

17   Despite these problems, the Venus flytrap remains a deadly threat to many bugs. Though the Venus flytrap may be a nice thing to look at, from a fly's point of view it's not a nice place to visit.

Did You Know?

Other carnivorous plants use different techniques to trap their prey.

- The pitcher plant forms traps shaped like cones. When something falls into one of these traps, it cannot crawl up the walls and get out.
- The sundew uses sticky nectar to attract bugs. Bugs that land on the nectar can't free themselves from it.
- The bladderwort grows in ponds and sucks in tiny organisms through a little door in its underwater sac.

---

bacteria (bak-tir'-ē-ə) single-celled life-forms that sometimes cause disease

Ask Questions

Reread the questions you wrote on pages 45 and 46. Which questions are answered in the text? Write the answers on a separate sheet of paper.

Did you ask any questions that are **not** answered in the text? If so, where could you look to find the information that would answer each question? Write your answers on a separate sheet of paper.

Self-Check

Look back at the question you wrote on page 41.
- Does the information in the text answer your question? If it does, what is the answer? If it does not, where could you look to find more information?

Now look back at the prediction you wrote on page 42.
- Does your prediction match the text? Why or why not?

Write your answers on a separate sheet of paper.

Understanding What You Read

Fill in the circle next to the correct answer. You may look back at the text to help you choose the correct answers.

1. What problem do Venus flytraps solve by eating bugs?
    - ○ A. The plant's leaves sometimes begin to rot.
    - ○ B. The plant's traps don't always close completely.
    - ○ C. The plants don't get enough nourishment from the soil.

2. The diagram titled "Parts of the Venus Flytrap" helps support the author's point that
    - ○ A. the leaf of the trap is hinged in the middle.
    - ○ B. a shift in fluid causes the trap's leaf to close.
    - ○ C. it takes several days for the plant to digest a bug.

3. When the trap closes, it
    - ○ A. doesn't seal completely shut right away.
    - ○ B. lets in wind and rain to clean it.
    - ○ C. uses up all of its energy.

4. Which step has to happen **before** a Venus flytrap can properly digest a bug?
    - ○ A. The insect's shell is removed from the trap.
    - ○ B. The halves of the leaf form an airtight seal.
    - ○ C. The plant waits for a new trap to grow.

5. How is a bug an example of a necessity for the Venus flytrap?
    - ○ A. Bugs are attracted to the sweet-smelling nectar of the Venus flytrap's leaves.
    - ○ B. Bugs provide important nutrients for the Venus flytrap.
    - ○ C. Smaller bugs can escape from the Venus flytrap.

Score 4 points for each correct answer.

_____ /20   **Total Score: Activity A**

Asking Questions

Paragraph 12 from the article is shown below. Read the paragraph. Then use the paragraph to complete the activities.

> Because the trap doesn't seal shut immediately, smaller bugs can still crawl out. Digesting prey requires energy, and it's not worthwhile for the plant to spend energy to digest prey unless the prey will provide plenty of energy in return. Larger bugs provide more energy, so the plant makes sure they can't get out. As they thrash around and try to escape, they touch the trigger hairs again, causing the leaf to close entirely. Within just a few minutes, the halves of the leaf form an airtight seal.

1. Read each question below. Then fill in the circle next to the question that is answered in the paragraph above.

   ○ A. What is the purpose of the airtight seal?
   ○ B. Why does the trap let smaller bugs escape?
   ○ C. How much energy does the plant use to digest food?

2. Write a new question about the paragraph above. The answer to this question should **not** be given in the paragraph text. Then write **two** ways you could find the answer on your own.

Question _____

_____

Two Ways I Could Find the Answer

1. _____

_____

2. _____

_____

Score 5 points each for numbers 1 and 2.

_____ /10   **Total Score: Activity B**

Using Words

Follow the instructions below. Write your answers on the lines.

1. List **three** animals that are **predators.**

_____

_____

_____

2. List **two** questions that scientists might find **intriguing.**

_____

_____

3. List **two** reasons that people might add a **supplement** to their diets.

_____

_____

4. List **three** things that are **edible** for humans.

_____

_____

_____

5. List **two** things that might cause a person to feel **vulnerable.**

_____

_____

Score 4 points for each correct answer.

_____ /20 **Total Score: Activity C**

Writing About It

Write a Comic Strip Write a comic strip about a Venus flytrap catching and eating a fly. Finish the caption sentence in each panel to write your comic strip. Be sure your writing matches the information in the text. Use the checklist on page 119 to check your work.

A fly draws near a Venus flytrap, attracted to _____ _____

The fly sets off the trap by _____ _____

The trap does not seal shut right away, but the cilia stop _____ _____

After the leaves of the trap form an airtight seal, the plant _____ _____

Lesson 4 Add your scores from activities A, B, and C to get your total score.

_____ **A** Understanding What You Read
_____ **B** Asking Questions
_____ **C** Using Words
_____ **Total Score**   Multiply your **Total Score x 2** _____
                                    This is your percentage score.
              Record your percentage score on the graph on page 121.

MUDSLIDES
MUD ON THE MOVE

Mudslides can cause
massive destruction of
property and lives.

READING SKILL **Understanding Line Graphs**

Authors sometimes include **line graphs** with the text. Line graphs help readers see how things change in relation to each other. Most line graphs show how things change over time. A line graph's *x* axis, or horizontal axis, shows units of time. The *y* axis, or vertical axis, shows what is changing.

EXAMPLE

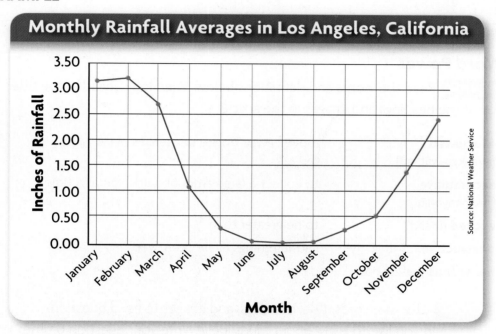

Monthly Rainfall Averages in Los Angeles, California

Source: National Weather Service

This line graph shows the average monthly rainfall in Los Angeles, California. You can get a lot of information by looking at how the line rises and falls. For example, you can see that the line is at its highest point in February. This means that February is usually the rainiest month in Los Angeles.

Look closely at the line on the graph. Then write the words *more rain* or *less rain* on each line below to explain what the graph shows.

In Los Angeles, August usually gets _____ than September.

In Los Angeles, January usually gets _____ than June.

In Los Angeles, November usually gets _____ than April.

Getting Ready to Read

Think About What You Know

CONNECT Think about how dirt turns into mud on a rainy day. What do you know about mud and mudslides? Write your answer here.

_____

_____

_____

Word Power

PREVIEW Read the words and definitions below. Then look ahead at the title and at the headings and images in the article.

evacuated (i-va'-kyə-wāt'-əd)	moved away from a dangerous place
accumulate (ə-kū'-myə-lāt')	to collect a large amount a little bit at a time
exceed (ik-sēd')	to be greater than
destructive (di-strək'-tiv)	causing things to be destroyed
hazardous (ha'-zər-dəs)	dangerous

QUESTION Use the words, title, headings, and images to ask a question. What would you like to know about mudslides? Write your question on the lines below.

_____

_____

_____

Reason to Read

Read to find out if the information in the text answers your question. At the end of the article, you will be asked to look back at your question. You will decide whether or not your question is answered in the text.

MUDSLIDES
MUD ON THE MOVE

1   As rescue workers **evacuated** hundreds of homeowners from a small California town, people could hear the terrifying sounds of their homes being crushed behind them.

2   You might think that only earthquakes, tornadoes, and hurricanes are capable of destroying houses. But how about mud? Mudslides, which are also a dangerous force of nature, are responsible for death and destruction all over the world.

The Ground Beneath Your Feet

3   A mudslide is a type of fast-moving landslide. Landslides occur on slopes that are typically made of loose material such as soil, rocks, or other **debris.** This loose material rests on a solid bottom layer of very hard rock called bedrock. A landslide occurs when large quantities of the loose material slide down the slope.

4   But most of the time, two forces hold the loose material on the slope. One force is **gravity.** This might surprise you, because gravity also causes landslides. Gravity pulls everything toward the center of the earth, so anything on a slope actually gets pulled down from different angles. This means that while gravity is pulling the material *down* the slope, it is also pulling the material *into* the slope and toward the bedrock.

debris (də-brē′) the pieces of something that has been broken
gravity (gra′-və-tē) the force that pulls one body of matter toward another

Predict

Reread the shaded text. This sentence talks about when landslides occur. Use this information to make a prediction. What will you learn about what causes landslides? Write your prediction on the lines below.

_____

_____

_____

_____

How did what you already know help you make your prediction?

_____

_____

_____

55

5   The other force is friction, which happens when one surface rubs against another. Soil particles rub against each other and against the bedrock, holding the soil in place. To get a sense of how friction works, press your palms together as hard as you can. Keep one hand in place and slowly drag the other hand downward without lessening the pressure. It's hard to move your hand, isn't it? Think of the hand that's not moving as bedrock and of the other hand as soil, and you will get an idea of how friction keeps soil from sliding easily.

6   But if such powerful forces hold soil in place, what would ever cause it to move down the slope?

Shifting Ground

7   Three factors can tip the balance of forces enough to cause a landslide. One has to do with the makeup of the soil. Sometimes the soil resting on the bedrock is dense, which helps keep it from moving too easily. But soil that is filled with holes doesn't allow for much friction, so it's more likely to slide.

8   A second factor is the natural movement of material on the slope. This can occur from freezing and thawing, or from an underground shift that moves the land above it. It can also happen when **vegetation** is removed by fire or drought. The roots of trees and plants help anchor soil in place; when these roots are gone, the soil's movement increases and makes the downward pull stronger.

9   It's not just nature that contributes to landslides—human activity, the third factor, plays a role as well. When people cut into the earth to build roads or chop down trees to collect logs, it upsets the balance that keeps the soil from moving. And constructing buildings on slopes adds weight to the soil, which causes it to shift.

Predict

Review the "Shifting Ground" section. Then look back at the prediction you wrote on page 55. Does your prediction match the text? Why or why not?

_____

_____

_____

Mudslides can sometimes cause roads to collapse. **Think about other ways mudslides can make certain roads dangerous.**

vegetation (veʹ-jə-tāʹ-shən) the plant life of an area

Rain, Rain, Go Away

10   What distinguishes a mudslide from other types of landslides is the role water plays in causing it. When the soil on a slope gets soaked, it turns into mud. But just a little moisture doesn't trigger a mudslide. What's needed is a massive amount of water for the soil to turn into a gooey, moving mess—like cake batter pouring out of a bowl.

11   So where does this massive amount of water come from? One of the most common causes is extremely heavy rainfall, especially from tropical storms or hurricanes. In 1998 Hurricane Mitch dumped about 75 inches (190.5 cm) of rain over parts of Central America, producing deadly mudslides that swept away whole villages. And in 1994, two months after wildfires swept through mountains in Colorado and destroyed the vegetation, heavy rains caused several mudslides in the area.

12   Rain is not the only thing that can soak the soil enough to cause a mudslide. Earthquakes can squeeze up underground water to soak a slope's soil, and hot lava from a volcano can melt enough snow and ice to turn soil into thick mud.

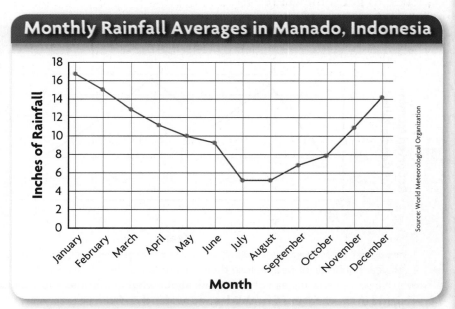

Monthly Rainfall Averages in Manado, Indonesia

Source: World Meteorological Organization

The city of Manado in Indonesia has been hit very hard by mudslides at various times. The amount of rainfall the city gets in certain months is a big contributor to these mudslides. **Think about which months of the year mudslides are most likely to occur in Manado.**

Use Line Graphs

Study the line graph titled "Monthly Rainfall Averages in Manado, Indonesia." How much more rain does Manado get in May than in July? Fill in the circle next to the correct answer.

○ ten times more
○ three times more
○ two times more

Moving Mud

13   As water soaks through the soil, it goes down toward the bedrock. Water cannot pass through some types of bedrock; unless there are cracks in the bedrock for the water to drain through, it continues to **accumulate.** It ends up collecting in the space where the soil meets the bedrock, creating what is known as a slip plane. This means that the water lubricates, or reduces friction, in this area, freeing the heavy, wet soil to plunge downhill.

14   As the mud heads downhill, it picks up more material, gaining power and speed as it goes. A typical mudslide moves at about 10 **miles per hour** (mph), but the more powerful ones can **exceed** 35 mph. That's the speed of a car driving down a city street!

Path of Destruction

15   Mudslides do a lot more than make everything in their path wet and dirty. They occur all over the world, from Japan to Pakistan to Italy to Nicaragua, and wherever they occur, their effects are often deadly and **destructive.** Because mudslides can happen so quickly and are so powerful, people have little or no time to get somewhere safe.

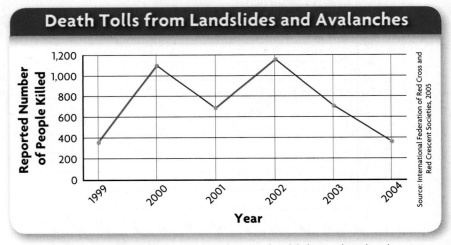

Death Tolls from Landslides and Avalanches

Source: International Federation of Red Cross and Red Crescent Societies, 2005

Each year hundreds of people lose their lives to landslides and avalanches, which involve snow instead of soil. **Think about what conditions could cause changes in the number of landslides and avalanches from year to year.**

miles per hour (mīlz′-pər-owr′) how fast something goes; how many miles something moves in an hour

Use Line Graphs

Study the line graph titled "Death Tolls from Landslides and Avalanches." How many more landslide and avalanche deaths occurred in 2001 than in 1999? Fill in the circle next to the correct answer.

- ⭘ about 150 more
- ⭘ about 350 more
- ⭘ about 650 more

Finish the sentence below to compare the death tolls of three of the years.

In _____
more people died than

in _____

and _____
combined.

16   The **Red Cross** estimates that in the United States, mudslides and landslides cause 25 to 50 deaths each year. In other parts of the world, the death tolls can be much more alarming. For example, in 1985 a volcano erupted in Colombia, creating a mudslide so immense it wiped out a city nearly 46 miles (74 km) away. Parts of the city were buried under more than 100 feet (30 meters) of mud, and more than 23,000 people died.

17   In addition to the loss of life, the physical destruction is astounding. In the United States alone, the Red Cross estimates that mudslides may cause $2 billion in property damage each year. And recovery for an area hit by a mudslide may take a long time. For example, a mudslide may release waste into an area's drinking water, making it unsafe to live there for quite a while.

Safety Measures

18   Although mudslides often strike quickly, there may be some warning signs. Bulges in walls, cracks in sidewalks, and fences tilting at strange angles aren't necessarily signs that a mudslide is happening, but they are signs that the ground is shifting. The clearest and most immediate warning sign is the rumbling sound of wet earth as it begins to descend from a nearby slope.

19   If a mudslide is coming, you should run to higher ground or seek shelter in the strongest building you can find. Mudslides may not be the most destructive force of nature, but they are extremely **hazardous** and need to be taken seriously.

Think about how building a house on the edge of a slope can contribute to landslides.

Self-Check
Look back at the question you wrote on page 54.
- Does the information in the text answer your question? If it does, what is the answer? If it does not, where could you look to find more information?

Write your answers on a separate sheet of paper.

Red Cross (red'-krôs') an international organization that provides relief to victims of war and natural disasters

Understanding What You Read

Fill in the circle next to the correct answer. You may look back at the text to help you choose the correct answers.

1. Sometimes the soil resting on the bedrock is dense, which helps keep it from
   - ○ A. absorbing water.
   - ○ B. moving too easily.
   - ○ C. holding up buildings.

2. What is one effect of cutting down trees?
   - ○ A. It increases the chances of rainfall.
   - ○ B. It takes away roots that hold soil in place.
   - ○ C. It makes soil resting on bedrock very firm.

3. Which of these **best** summarizes the information in the "Moving Mud" section?
   - ○ A. The water that collects between the soil and the bedrock causes the mud to slide downhill with increasing speed.
   - ○ B. Water cannot pass through some types of bedrock, so it collects in the space where the soil meets the bedrock.
   - ○ C. Water causes the mud to head downhill as fast as a car drives down a street.

4. From the information in the article, you can infer that
   - ○ A. human activity causes more landslides than storms do.
   - ○ B. mudslides are more dangerous than tornadoes or earthquakes.
   - ○ C. hilly, rainy areas experience more mudslides than flat, dry areas do.

5. Under which heading would you be **most likely** to find information about how to protect yourself during a mudslide?
   - ○ A. Rain, Rain, Go Away
   - ○ B. Path of Destruction
   - ○ C. Safety Measures

Score 4 points for each correct answer.

_____/20 **Total Score: Activity A**

Understanding Line Graphs

One of the line graphs from the article is shown below. Study the line graph. Then use the line graph to complete the activities.

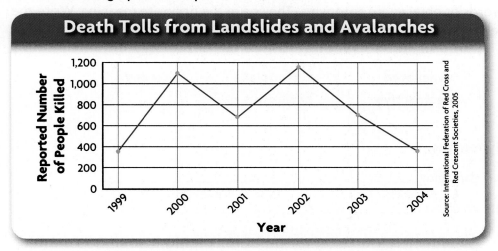

Death Tolls from Landslides and Avalanches

Source: International Federation of Red Cross and Red Crescent Societies, 2005

1. From the information in the graph, which of these statements is true?
    ○ A. In 2001 about twice as many people died as in 1999.
    ○ B. In 2004 about twice as many people died as in 2003.
    ○ C. In 2003 about twice as many people died as in 2000.

2. Use the information in the line graph to write a paragraph. Your paragraph should explain what the graph says about the death tolls from landslides and avalanches. Complete the sentences below to write your paragraph.

    In _____ fewer people died as a result of landslides

    and avalanches than in _____. The year the most

    people died is _____. The year the fewest people died

    is _____. About the same amount of people died in

    _____ and _____.

Score 5 points each for numbers 1 and 2.
_____ /10 **Total Score: Activity B**

Using Words

The words and phrases in the list below relate to the words in the box. Some words or phrases in the list are synonyms. They have the same meaning. Some words or phrases are antonyms. They have the opposite meaning. Write the related word from the box on each line. Use each word from the box **twice.**

evacuated	**accumulate**	**exceed**
destructive	**hazardous**	

Synonyms

1. damaging _____

2. go above _____

3. pile up _____

4. risky _____

5. escaped from a harmful area _____

Antonyms

6. dwindle _____

7. stayed somewhere despite a threat _____

8. safe _____

9. creative _____

10. drop below _____

Score 2 points for each correct answer.

_____ /20   **Total Score: Activity C**

Writing About It

Write a Postcard Suppose you have traveled to a town recently hit by a mudslide to help people clean up and repair damages. Write a postcard to a friend. Tell your friend about the mudslide. Finish the sentences below to write your postcard. Be sure your writing matches the information in the text. Use the checklist on page 119 to check your work.

Dear _____

Today I'm in a small town in the hills helping people

recover from a mudslide. A mudslide is _____

_____

This area had received a lot of rain for several days, and

all that water _____

_____

It is lucky that no one was killed. Sometimes people don't

have a chance to escape because mudslides _____

_____

    Sincerely,

_____

_____
456 Muddy Way
Anytown, State 54321

Lesson 5 Add your scores from activities A, B, and C to get your total score.

_____ **A** Understanding What You Read

_____ **B** Understanding Line Graphs

_____ **C** Using Words

_____ **Total Score**

        Multiply your **Total Score x 2** _____

           This is your percentage score.

      Record your percentage score on the graph on page 121.

MOSQUITOES
Big Trouble in a Little Package

Mosquitoes rely on the blood they suck from humans and other animals.

READING SKILL **Drawing Conclusions**

Good readers **draw conclusions.** Conclusions are general statements that are based on information in the text. As you read, pay attention to the details in the text. Combine these details with what you already know to come up with a larger idea that is not stated in the text. To draw conclusions, ask yourself this question: *What larger idea is the author trying to get across to readers?*

EXAMPLE

> Most people are eager to keep mosquitoes away, but not everyone agrees about the best way to do this. Some people use sprays or lotions that contain chemicals. Others prefer more natural methods, such as putting peppermint oil on the skin.

One conclusion you could draw from the example paragraph above is that *mosquitoes don't like the smell of peppermint.* There are two clues in the text that support this conclusion. The clues are written in the flowchart below. How does what you already know support this conclusion? Write what you already know in the box below.

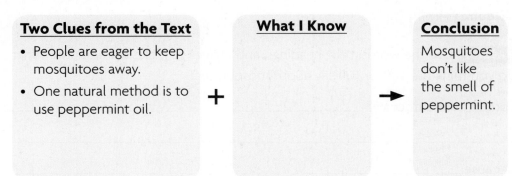

Two Clues from the Text

- People are eager to keep mosquitoes away.
- One natural method is to use peppermint oil.

+

What I Know

→

Conclusion

Mosquitoes don't like the smell of peppermint.

Getting Ready to Read

Think About What You Know

CONNECT   Think about what may cause mosquitoes to bite people. Have you ever been bitten by a mosquito? What do you know about mosquitoes? Write your answers here.

_____

_____

_____

Word Power

PREVIEW   Read the words and definitions below. Then look ahead at the title and at the headings and images in the article.

equipped (i-kwipt')	having the things that are needed
exhale (eks-hāl')	to breathe out
infected (in-fekt'-əd)	affected by germs that cause disease
fatal (fā'-təl)	deadly
acquire (ə-kwīr')	to get

PREDICT   Use the words, title, headings, and images to make a prediction. What do you think the author will say about mosquitoes?

I predict the author will _____

_____

because _____

_____

Reason to Read

Read to find out if the prediction you wrote above matches the information in the text. At the end of the article, you will be asked about your prediction. You will need to explain how your prediction is the same as the text or different from it.

MOSQUITOES
Big Trouble in a Little Package

1   You're in your bed on a summer night. As you drift off to sleep, you hear a high-pitched buzz. It's getting closer, and soon it's right in your ear. It's a mosquito! You can't find the mosquito when you try to swat it, but it can find you. The buzzing stops, and you probably feel a tiny pinch. Tomorrow you'll have an itchy bump on your skin—the unwelcome mark of the mosquito.

2   Why do mosquitoes bite people? The short answer is that they want your blood. To understand *why* they want it, it helps to know how this little bug's body works.

"Little Fly"

3   There are more than 2,500 species of mosquito—which means "little fly" in Spanish—around the world. Mosquitoes vary in length from just 3/16 to 1/2 of an inch (4.8 to 12.7 mm). The males generally live for a week or two, while the females of some species can live up to a few months. During their life span, mosquitoes go through three stages of growth before they become adults.

4   Mosquitoes begin as eggs that are usually laid in puddles or other still water, such as in birdbaths. Although some eggs can take weeks to hatch, most hatch in two or three days. After hatching, a little wormlike creature called a larva wriggles free from the egg and hangs out just below the water's surface. It breathes through a tube on its tail, which sticks out of the water, and it feeds on floating bits of food.

My WORKSPACE

Still water can become a mosquito breeding ground. **Think about why mosquitoes prefer to breed in still water instead of running water.**

Predict

Reread the shaded text. Use this information to make a prediction. What will the author say about why mosquitoes want blood? Write your prediction on the lines below.

_____

_____

_____

_____

How did what you already know help you make your prediction?

_____

_____

_____

_____

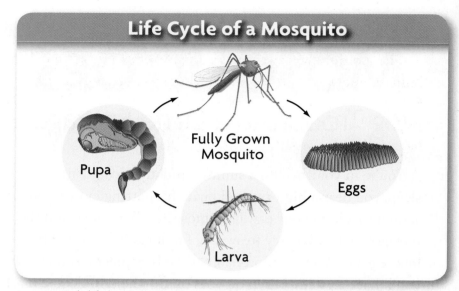

Life Cycle of a Mosquito

Fully Grown Mosquito

Pupa

Eggs

Larva

A mosquito's life begins as one of hundreds of eggs that have been laid in still water. **Think about why mosquitoes lay hundreds of eggs at a time.**

5   After a few days, the larva enters the third stage and becomes a pupa. The pupa stops eating, and its skin forms a cocoon around it while it finishes growing. After two or three days more, the cocoon splits open and releases the blood-hungry adult mosquito.

Ouch!

6   Well, not *all* mosquitoes look for blood; only female mosquitoes do. Males generally feed on fruit juices, but females need lots of protein to produce eggs—as many as 400 at a time! And blood just so happens to be packed with protein.

7   A mosquito bites by sticking her proboscis—a needlelike tube extending from the front of her head—under the skin of her prey. Because the proboscis is hollow, like a straw, the mosquito can suck the blood from her prey. To make her job easier, the mosquito's **saliva** contains a chemical that prevents blood from clotting. (When you get a cut, special blood cells form a seal, or clot, inside the cut to stop the flow of blood.) If blood can't clot properly, the mosquito can continue drinking it until she's had her fill or until she's swatted.

Predict

Reread **paragraph 6**. Then look back at the prediction you wrote on page 67. Does your prediction match the text? Why or why not?

_____

_____

_____

_____

saliva (sə-lī′-və) a liquid that is produced in the mouth; spit

8   The mosquito always leaves some of her saliva behind. The human body's **immune system** recognizes this saliva as a foreign substance, so it sends cells to attack it. When these cells rush to the saliva, they create a raised bump on your skin. This bump, commonly called a "mosquito bite," itches like crazy until your cells have broken down the saliva's substances.

The Hunter and the Hunted

9   Since these bites are so unpleasant, it's best to just stay out of a mosquito's way, right? That's easier said than done. Unfortunately for us, mosquitoes are perfectly **equipped** to find prey. They usually target **warm-blooded** animals, such as birds, people, and other mammals. Numerous sensors on their heads—including two antennae—help them detect and zero in on suitable victims.

10   Like many hunters, mosquitoes use vision to locate prey. Their vision isn't quite like ours, but it does allow them to see the contrast, or difference, between light and dark shades. Mosquitoes are drawn to darker shades, so they're more likely to bite someone wearing dark clothing than someone wearing light clothing. They can also spot motion. If something is moving, they know it is alive and is probably suitable prey.

11   But mosquitoes don't rely on sight alone. They're also able to sense certain chemicals that prey send out from their bodies. For example, mosquitoes can detect carbon dioxide, a gas that animals and people **exhale.** Lactic acid, a chemical produced in our muscles and released in our breath and sweat, also attracts mosquitoes.

immune system (i-mūn'-sis'-təm) the group of body parts that fight illness and disease
warm-blooded (wôrm'-blə'-dəd) having a high body temperature that stays the same no matter what the surrounding temperature is

Draw Conclusions
Reread **paragraph 8.** Fill in the circle next to the conclusion that is **best** supported by the text.
- ○ Some mosquitoes don't leave any saliva behind.
- ○ The itching of the bump means healing is taking place.
- ○ The immune system blocks mosquitoes from getting blood.

What clues or details from the text support your conclusion? Write **two** clues or details here.

1. _____
_____

2. _____
_____

Think about why, for a mosquito, a proboscis is better for getting blood than a mouth would be.

12   Maybe you've noticed that mosquitoes are more likely to bite some people than others. Lactic acid offers one explanation; the more a person sweats, the more chemical signals that person sends to mosquitoes. Mosquitoes can also detect body heat. This would explain why most mosquitoes target warm-blooded creatures, such as people, much more than cold-blooded creatures, such as reptiles.

13   If the worst thing that could happen when a mosquito finds you is an itchy bump and a tiny bit of blood loss, it wouldn't be that big a deal. Sadly, however, mosquitoes can cause much more damage than that.

More Than Just Annoying

14   Sometimes a mosquito bite leads to serious illness or even death. That's because mosquitoes can carry diseases. If a mosquito bites a person or an animal **infected** with a disease, she can pick up the disease-causing **viruses** or bacteria and pass them on when she bites another victim.

15   One of the most widespread and sometimes **fatal** of these diseases is an infection known as malaria. Although malaria is largely limited to tropical regions—such as various countries in Africa, Asia, and Central and South America—it infects about 400 million people every year. Some estimates place its death toll at more than half a million people per year.

16   There are several other deadly diseases spread by mosquitoes. One of them is the West Nile virus, which has drawn a lot of attention in the United States in recent years. Between 1999, when it first appeared in the United States, and 2006, the virus was responsible for more than 900 deaths.

Draw Conclusions

Reread the shaded text. One conclusion you could draw from the text is that *malaria can be very difficult to prevent and cure.*

What clues or details from the text support this conclusion? Write **two** clues or details here.

1. _____

_____

2. _____

_____

How does what you already know support this conclusion?

_____

_____

_____

_____

viruses (vī'-rəs-əs) very small things that can invade the body and cause disease

West Nile Virus in the United States

Source: Centers for Disease Control and Prevention, ©2007

Think about what the reasons might have been for the sharp increase in confirmed cases from 2001 to 2003 and for the sudden drop in 2004.

17   But while many people in the United States have gotten diseases from mosquito bites, often they are fine after they receive medical treatment. And **vaccinations** are very helpful in protecting people from getting many of these diseases in the first place. Also, people try to control mosquito populations by draining areas of standing water and spraying chemicals on mosquito breeding grounds.

Protect Yourself

18   Because of vaccinations and medical treatments, chances are good that someone in the United States won't **acquire** a serious disease from a mosquito bite. However, it's still a good idea to protect yourself. Using an insect repellent helps keep mosquitoes away. And staying inside during dawn and dusk is a good idea, because this is when mosquitoes are most active. But no matter what you do, it's almost impossible to avoid every hungry mosquito. When you do get bitten, it helps to wash the tiny wound immediately to clean off germs that could infect it.

19   Mosquitoes are not bad news for all living things. They are an important food source for animals such as frogs, bats, and fish. But for humans, as you've read, this little pest can be very dangerous. So avoid these bugs whenever possible, and remember to take care of yourself if you cross paths with a mosquito.

vaccinations (vak′-sə-nā′-shənz) medicines that protect living things from disease

Draw Conclusions
Reread the shaded text. Using the clues and details in the text, what conclusion can you draw about the best ways to protect yourself from mosquitoes? Write your conclusion here.

_____

_____

_____

_____

How does what you already know support this conclusion?

_____

_____

_____

_____

Self-Check
Look back at the prediction you wrote on page 66.
• Does your prediction match the text? Why or why not?
Write your answers on a separate sheet of paper.

Understanding What You Read

Fill in the circle next to the correct answer. You may look back at the text to help you choose the correct answers.

1. What does a mosquito have to do **before** she can produce eggs?
   - ○ A. She has to feed on fruit juices.
   - ○ B. She has to drink a lot of blood.
   - ○ C. She has to grow to more than ½ of an inch long.

2. If blood can't clot properly, the mosquito
   - ○ A. can continue drinking it.
   - ○ B. does not get enough protein.
   - ○ C. will try biting something else.

3. Mosquitoes and hunters are similar because they both
   - ○ A. sense chemicals that come from prey.
   - ○ B. use their vision to locate prey.
   - ○ C. are drawn to darker shades.

4. The line graph titled "West Nile Virus in the United States" helps support the author's point that
   - ○ A. The disease existed in the United States in 1999.
   - ○ B. It is almost impossible to avoid every mosquito.
   - ○ C. Insect repellents help keep mosquitoes away.

5. How does draining areas of standing water help solve mosquito problems?
   - ○ A. It makes mosquitoes less active at dusk and dawn.
   - ○ B. It removes a common source of protein for mosquitoes.
   - ○ C. It limits the number of places where mosquito eggs can hatch.

Score 4 points for each correct answer.

_____/20   **Total Score: Activity A**

Drawing Conclusions

Paragraph 12 from the article is shown below. Read the paragraph. Then use the paragraph to complete the activities.

Maybe you've noticed that mosquitoes are more likely to bite some people than others. Lactic acid offers one explanation; the more a person sweats, the more chemical signals that person sends to mosquitoes. Mosquitoes can also detect body heat. This would explain why most mosquitoes target warm-blooded creatures, such as people, much more than cold-blooded creatures, such as reptiles.

1. Which conclusion is **best** supported by the clues and details in the text?
    ○ A. Most reptiles don't produce sweat or lactic acid.
    ○ B. Reptiles get bitten by mosquitoes more often than people do.
    ○ C. People attract more mosquitoes if they've just been running instead of sitting still.

2. What clues or details from the text support this conclusion? How does what you already know support this conclusion? Write **two** clues or details from the text and what you already know.

    Clue or Detail _____

    Clue or Detail _____

    What I Know _____

    _____

Using Words

Complete each sentence with a word from the box. Write the missing word on the line.

equipped	exhale	infected
fatal	acquire	

1. This truck is _____ with special tires that help it handle dangerous road conditions.

2. He plans to _____ a new hat and a new coat on his shopping trip.

3. When she swims underwater, she always tries to _____ before she rises to the surface.

4. His decision to sail into the center of the storm was a _____ and tragic mistake.

5. Because I didn't wash the knee scrape I got when I fell down, the wound became _____ .

Choose one word from the box. Write a new sentence using the word. Be sure to put at least one detail in your sentence. The detail should show that you understand what the word means. Use the sentences above as examples.

6. _____

   _____

Writing About It

Write a Journal Entry Suppose you are visiting a tropical region where there are many mosquitoes. Write a journal entry about this experience. Finish the sentences below to write your journal entry. Be sure your writing matches the information in the text. Use the checklist on page 119 to check your work.

I love the warm weather here, but I sure don't love the mosquitoes! I've

learned that the only mosquitoes that bite are the _____

They bite people because _____

_____

_____

There are many puddles and wet places here that the mosquitoes use for _____

_____

_____

I have learned that it's smart to avoid mosquitoes because they can _____

_____

_____

I am trying to avoid the mosquitoes by _____

_____

_____

Lesson 6 Add your scores from activities A, B, and C to get your total score.

_____ **A** Understanding What You Read
_____ **B** Drawing Conclusions
_____ **C** Using Words
_____ **Total Score**

Multiply your **Total Score x 2** _____

This is your percentage score.

Record your percentage score on the graph on page 121.

Compare and Contrast

You read three articles about nature in Unit Two. Think about the topic of each article. Then choose **two** of the articles. Write the titles of the articles in the chart below. In the left and right columns, write ways that the two topics are different. In the center column, write the ways that they are similar.

Title _____	Similarities	Title _____

Use the chart above to write a summary of how these nature topics are alike and different. Finish the sentences below to write your summary.

_____ and _____ are different

because _____

_____

_____ and _____ are similar

because _____

_____

Unit 3

Technology

Cell Phones

Global Positioning System

Search Engines

Global Positioning System

Where in the World Am I?

The Global Positioning System
çan find your location just
about anywhere on Earth.

READING SKILL | Reviewing the Reading Skills

You practiced three reading skills in Unit One. Rate your understanding of each skill using the chart below. Use the following rating scale:

3 I understand this skill well. I use it easily and correctly while I read.

2 I understand this skill a little bit. I sometimes use it correctly while I read.

1 I don't understand this skill. I am not able to use it while I read.

Mark the box under the number 3, 2, or 1 for each skill.

	3	2	1	Need to review?		Turn to:
Making Predictions				Yes	No	Lesson 1, page 3
Making Connections				Yes	No	Lesson 2, page 15
Visualizing				Yes	No	Lesson 3, page 27

If you rated your understanding of a skill at 2 or 1, look back at the lesson page where that skill was taught. The lesson page is shown in the chart above. Reread the skill definition and the example. This will help you get ready to complete the next lesson.

After you have reviewed the skills, complete the sentences below.

The skill I find most helpful when reading is _____

because _____

_____

During this lesson, one thing I can do to improve my reading is _____

_____

_____

Getting Ready to Read

Think About What You Know

CONNECT Think of a time when you got lost. Perhaps you were on a nature hike or in a car with someone. How did you find your way again? Write your answer here.

_____

_____

_____

Word Power

PREVIEW Read the words and definitions below. Then look ahead at the title and at the headings and images in the article.

intersect (in′-tər-sekt′)	to meet and cross at a common point
calculate (kal′-kyə-lāt′)	to use numbers and math to find something out
synchronized (sing′-krə-nīzd′)	made to happen at the same time
spheres (sfirz)	ball-like shapes with all surface points at the same distance from a center point
monitoring (mä′-nə-tər-ing)	carefully watching or checking a thing or situation to see how it changes over time

PREDICT Use the words, title, headings, and images to make a prediction. What do you think the author will say about the Global Positioning System?

I predict the author will _____

_____

because _____

_____

Reason to Read

Read to find out if the prediction you wrote above matches the information in the text. At the end of the article, you will be asked about your prediction. You will need to explain how your prediction is the same as the text or different from it.

Global Positioning System
Where in the World Am I?

1   The fire began in a remote section of a national park. A park ranger spotted smoke, and a plane was sent to investigate. The pilot saw the blaze spreading fast. Thanks to special equipment aboard the plane, however, the pilot was able to direct firefighters to specific locations where they could fight the fire safely and effectively.

2   What was this special equipment aboard the plane? It was a Global Positioning System, or GPS, receiver. Let's take a look at how this remarkable navigation tool works.

Messages from Space

3   *Global* means "including or affecting the whole world." The Global Positioning System can pinpoint a person's location anywhere on Earth within a few yards or meters. It works day and night and in any kind of weather. You could be sailing across the Pacific Ocean, standing atop Mount Everest, or just driving down a neighborhood street. What makes this possible is satellite technology.

4   Satellite technology involves human-made devices that send and receive signals. These devices are launched into space, where they orbit, or circle, Earth much like the moon does, only closer. The GPS includes 24 main satellites that each orbit Earth once every 12 hours, or twice per day. The satellites are about 12,000 miles (19,312 km) above Earth, and they travel more than 7,000 miles (11,265 km) per hour.

81

Predict

Reread **paragraphs 5** and **6**. Use this information to make a prediction. What will the author say about the specific type of information the satellites send to the receivers?

_____

_____

_____

_____

What clues from the text helped you make your prediction?

_____

_____

_____

_____

5　The satellites send a constant stream of information to Earth using radio signals. To receive and use these signals, a person needs to have a GPS receiver. GPS receivers are like miniature computers designed to detect, decode, and process the signals. Receivers have a screen that displays information, and they are so small and light that they can be carried in your hand. They can also be installed in cars, trucks, airplanes, ships, and even submarines. How do the receivers tell you where you are?

Lost and Found

6　If a GPS receiver knows where several satellites are and how far each one is from where you are, then it can figure out your location. Let's take a look at a simple example.

7　Suppose you're traveling through an unfamiliar state and you get lost. When you stop to ask for help, one person tells you that you are 150 miles (241 km) from Red City. That means you are somewhere on the **perimeter** of a circle with Red City in the center and a **radius** of 150 miles. When you ask another person, you find out that you are 180 miles (290 km) from Green City. Imagine a second circle with a radius of 180 miles.

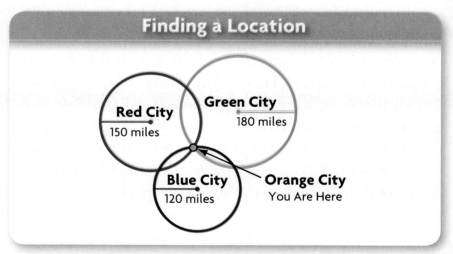

Finding a Location

Red City
150 miles

Green City
180 miles

Blue City
120 miles

Orange City
You Are Here

Think about the role math plays in finding the location of Orange City.

perimeter (pə-ri′-mə-tər) the outer boundary, or border, of a shape
radius (rā′-dē-əs) the distance between the center point and the **perimeter** of a circle

8   As the illustration on page 82 shows, the red and green circles **intersect** in two places. This means that your location is one of these two intersections. So you ask a third person, who says you are 120 miles (193 km) from Blue City. This information provides a third circle that will intersect with the other two circles in only one place. That is where you are—Orange City.

9   GPS works the same way, except that instead of having to **calculate** the distance from three cities, the receiver calculates the distance from three or four satellites. How does it do this?

Radio Signals

10   As you recall, the satellites send out radio signals. These radio signals travel at the speed of light, or roughly 186,000 miles (300,000 km) per second. That's really fast! Still, some time does pass between the moment a radio wave leaves a satellite and the moment it reaches a GPS receiver.

11   Each satellite continuously sends out three pieces of information. The first is a code number that identifies which satellite the signal came from. The satellite also sends its exact location. Because the orbits are predictable—they maintain the same course and travel at a constant speed—each satellite can be programmed to know its own orbit.

12   The third thing the satellite tells a receiver is the exact time a signal was sent according to its atomic clock. Each satellite has an atomic clock, which is much more accurate than a regular clock. Atomic clocks don't use moving parts; instead, they measure time based on the decay of atoms and the laws of nature. So travel times can be measured in fractions of a second.

Some GPS receivers are built right into cars and other vehicles. **Think about why it might be helpful to have a GPS receiver while driving to a new place.**

Predict

Reread **paragraphs 11** and **12.** Then look back at the prediction you wrote on page 82. Does your prediction match the text? Why or why not?

_____

_____

_____

_____

_____

_____

Connect
Use the information on this page to make a connection. Complete the sentence below.

When I read about _____

_____

_____

it reminds me _____

_____

_____

because _____

_____

_____

The user of this handheld receiver can see his or her location on a map that is programmed into it. **Think about another way a GPS receiver could tell you where you are.**

GPS satellite orbits are set up so that no matter where you are, there are always at least four satellites within range to send you signals. **Think about the different technologies scientists had to invent and master before they could create working satellites.**

Time to Calculate

13   Once a GPS receiver has all this information, it compares the satellite's time to the time on its own clock, which is constantly **synchronized** to the satellites' atomic clocks. The receiver figures out the travel time and then multiplies it by 186,000 miles per second to find the exact distance to the satellite.

14   Remember how we found out you were in Orange City? The receiver applies the same method, but it uses **spheres** instead of circles. Using each calculated distance as a radius, the receiver draws imaginary spheres with each satellite's location in their centers. Then it locates the one point where all the spheres intersect. This is where you are!

15   If it has information from three satellites, the receiver's screen can show your location in **latitude** and **longitude**; if it has information from four satellites, it can also find your **altitude.** Some receivers show your visual location on a map that appears on the screen.

latitude (laʹ-tə-tōōdʹ) how far north or south you are from the equator, which is an imaginary line that divides Earth in half (top and bottom)
longitude (länʹ-jə-tōōdʹ) how far east or west you are from the prime meridian, which is an imaginary line through Greenwich, England, that divides Earth in half (left and right)
altitude (alʹ-tə-tōōdʹ) how high above sea level a thing or a place is

Quality Control

16　　In addition to the satellites and receivers, there is another important part of the GPS: **monitoring** stations. The purpose of these stations is to make sure that all the data that drives the GPS is accurate and up-to-date.

17　　At the monitoring stations, computers automatically collect data from the satellites and send it to the master control station on Schriever Air Force Base in Colorado. There GPS experts analyze the data and make any necessary adjustments. For example, because the satellites' orbits can be influenced by things such as the moon and the sun, the experts might have to update a satellite's exact position in space. Then large ground antennas send the updated information back to the satellite.

Many Uses

18　　The GPS is becoming more and more popular. In addition to being used in emergency situations, such as forest fires, handheld receivers help people find their way at night and in bad weather conditions such as blizzards. Many new cars come equipped with a GPS receiver, which shows an onscreen road map with a little dot that represents your location as you drive down the street.

19　　As the technology improves, GPS receivers become less and less expensive. Some people say that soon GPS receivers will be like cell phones: almost everyone will have one.

Did You Know?
- GPS technology was originally developed by the U.S. military to monitor the location of nuclear submarines. The U.S. military still controls and maintains the system; however, anyone in the world who has a receiver can use the GPS.
- The GPS is not the only global navigation satellite system in the world. Russia also operates a system, called GLONASS, and the European Union is in the process of creating a system called Galileo.

This is a GPS monitoring station located on the island of Hawaii. **Think about why GPS monitoring stations are necessary to keep GPS data accurate.**

Self-Check
Look back at the prediction you wrote on page 80.
- Does your prediction match the text? Why or why not?

Write your answers on a separate sheet of paper.

Understanding What You Read

Fill in the circle next to the correct answer. You may look back at the text to help you choose the correct answers.

1. If a GPS receiver knows where several satellites are and how far each one is from where you are, then it can
   - ○ A. figure out your location.
   - ○ B. operate without a clock.
   - ○ C. send out a radio signal.

2. The diagram titled "Finding a Location" helps support the author's point that GPS receivers
   - ○ A. can be installed in cars, trucks, and airplanes.
   - ○ B. need information from more than one satellite.
   - ○ C. show the users' locations right on their screens.

3. If you could rename the "Quality Control" section, which of these would be the **best** choice?
   - ○ A. The Role of GPS Experts
   - ○ B Why Satellite Orbits Change
   - ○ C. The Importance of Monitoring Stations

4. Using the GPS is different from using a paper map because only the GPS can
   - ○ A. be used while traveling by car.
   - ○ B. tell someone where he or she is.
   - ○ C. show the location of streets and towns.

5. From what the author told you about the GPS, you can conclude that it
   - ○ A. is a complex and carefully designed system.
   - ○ B. should only be used in emergency situations.
   - ○ C. can be very difficult and expensive to use.

Score 4 points for each correct answer.

_____/20 **Total Score: Activity A**

Making Connections and Visualizing

Paragraph 5 from the article is shown below. Read the paragraph. Then use the paragraph to complete the activities.

The satellites send a constant stream of information to Earth using radio signals. To receive and use these signals, a person needs to have a GPS receiver. GPS receivers are like miniature computers designed to detect, decode, and process the signals. Receivers have a screen that displays information, and they are so small and light that they can be carried in your hand. They can also be installed in cars, trucks, airplanes, ships, and even submarines. How do the receivers tell you where you are?

1. Complete the sentence to make a strong connection to the paragraph.

When I read about _____

_____

it reminds me _____

_____

because _____

_____

2. Use the details from the paragraph and what you already know to create a picture in your mind. Draw what you are visualizing in the box below.

Score 5 points each for numbers 1 and 2.

_____ /10 **Total Score: Activity B**

Using Words

Follow the instructions below. Write your answers on the lines.

1. List **two** things that might **intersect** a street.

   _____

   _____

2. List **two** tools that can be used to **calculate**.

   _____

   _____

3. List **two** things that can be **synchronized**.

   _____

   _____

4. List **three** things that are shaped like **spheres**.

   _____

   _____

   _____

5. List **two** things a scientist might do when **monitoring** a lab experiment.

   _____

   _____

Score 4 points for each correct answer.

_____ /20   **Total Score: Activity C**

Writing About It

Make a Prediction Use what you learned in the article and what you already know to make a prediction about new uses for the GPS in the future. Finish the sentences below to make your prediction. Be sure your writing matches the information in the text. Use the checklist on page 119 to check your work.

I predict that _____

_____

_____

One clue from the text that supports my prediction is _____

_____

_____

_____

Another clue from the text that supports my prediction is _____

_____

_____

_____

One thing I already know that supports my

prediction is _____

_____

_____

_____

Lesson 7 Add your scores from activities A, B, and C to get your total score.
_____ **A** Understanding What You Read
_____ **B** Making Connections and Visualizing
_____ **C** Using Words
_____ **Total Score**

Multiply your **Total Score x 2** _____
This is your percentage score.
Record your percentage score on the graph on page 121.

CELL PHONES
In Touch, On the Go

It's difficult today to go anywhere without seeing someone on a cell phone.

READING SKILL **Reviewing the Reading Skills**

You practiced three reading skills in Unit Two. Rate your understanding of each skill using the chart below. Use the following rating scale:

3 I understand this skill well. I use it easily and correctly while I read.

2 I understand this skill a little bit. I sometimes use it correctly while I read.

1 I don't understand this skill. I am not able to use it while I read.

Mark the box under the number 3, 2, or 1 for each skill.

	3	2	1	Need to review?		Turn to:
Asking Questions				Yes	No	Lesson 4, page 41
Line Graphs				Yes	No	Lesson 5, page 53
Drawing Conclusions				Yes	No	Lesson 6, page 65

If you rated your understanding of a skill at 2 or 1, look back at the lesson page where that skill was taught. The lesson page is shown in the chart above. Reread the skill definition and the example. This will help you get ready to complete the next lesson.

After you have reviewed the skills, complete the sentences below.

The skill I find most helpful when reading is _____

because _____

_____

During this lesson, one thing I can do to improve my reading is _____

_____

_____

Getting Ready to Read

Think About What You Know

CONNECT Think about how many people you know who use cell phones. What do you know about how cell phones work? Write your answer here.

_____

_____

_____

Word Power

PREVIEW Read the words and definitions below. Then look ahead at the title and at the headings and images in the article.

transmit (tranz-mit′)	to send from one place to another
mobile (mō′-bəl)	able to move around easily
typical (ti′-pi-kəl)	having the special features of a particular group
allotted (ə-lät′-əd)	given or assigned as a part of something
overlap (ō′-vər-lap′)	to extend over and cover up part of something else

QUESTION Use the words, title, headings, and images to ask a question. What would you like to know about cell phones? Write your question on the lines below.

_____

_____

_____

Reason to Read

Read to find out if the information in the text answers your question. At the end of the article, you will be asked to look back at your question. You will decide whether or not your question is answered in the text.

CELL PHONES
In Touch, On the Go

1   A young woman on a bus calls her workplace to say she's running late. An older man on a sidewalk calls a restaurant to ask for directions. A teenage boy in a grocery store hears his phone ring—it's his mother calling to remind him to buy milk.

2   People use cell phones in many places and for many reasons. These pocket-sized devices help keep people connected almost anyplace they go. But how does this wireless device work, and how in the world does a call find you when you're constantly on the move?

The Fabulous Phone

3   The cell phone is the perfect blend of two older, well-known technologies: the telephone and the radio. The telephone part is obvious, but the radio part might surprise you. A cell phone is part radio because it uses radio waves to work.

4   A traditional phone, with its **handset** attached to its base by a cord, transforms sounds into electrical signals. These signals then travel through wires to another person's phone. Cordless phones, which first became popular in the 1990s, work a little differently. Because there is no cord attached to the handset, cordless phones use radio waves to **transmit** signals back and forth between the handset and the base. The base then sends the electrical signals over the same telephone wires that traditional phones use. But a cordless phone has a very limited range. The handset often won't work if it goes beyond a couple hundred feet of the base.

Cell phones need an antenna to operate properly. Many cell phones hide the antenna inside the phone. **Think about why people might not like having an antenna sticking out of the phone.**

Ask Questions

Reread **paragraph 3.** What question would you like to ask about the information in this paragraph? Write your question here.

_____

_____

_____

How does asking this question help you set a purpose for reading?

_____

_____

_____

---

handset (hand'-set') the part of a telephone you talk into and listen from

Draw Conclusions

Reread the shaded text. Fill in the circle next to the conclusion that is **best** supported by the text.

○ The size of a cell depends on how many people in it will be using cell phones.

○ Cell phones work better in cities than in rural areas.

○ People in rural areas don't use cell phones very often.

What clues or details from the text support your conclusion? Write **two** clues or details here.

1. _____

   _____

2. _____

   _____

Sometimes cell towers are designed to look like trees so that they blend into the landscape. **Think about why some people might think it's important that the towers blend into the landscape.**

5   With cell phones, people aren't restricted by cords and wires or by a very limited range. Like a cordless phone, a cell phone transforms your voice to radio waves. But cell phones use antennas and towers instead of just telephone wires to send signals. Once the wires are out of the equation, you're free to be **mobile** and communicate at the same time.

The Cell

6   To understand how a cell phone functions, first you need to understand what is meant by a "cell." The *cell* in *cell phone* refers to a small, roughly circular **geographic** area. Often cells are about 10 square miles, but their sizes can vary. In rural areas where there aren't many users, a cell may be much larger; in more populated areas such as cities, a cell may be significantly smaller. Each cell contains a base station with a radio tower, which acts as an antenna. Because cell phones send their radio waves to these cell towers, the towers need to be set high above the ground. You can often see the towers on building roofs or on hillsides near highways. Some areas without a lot of people don't have these cell towers, so cell phones don't work there.

7   As you might expect, cell phones aren't the only devices that use radio waves. Radios (obviously), security systems, and baby monitors—to name just a few—use them too. Many different things can use radio waves without interfering with one another because radio waves have different **frequencies.**

8   However, there is a limited number of radio frequencies, so the various technologies that use them have to find a way to share the frequencies. To make sure there are enough to go around, the government determines which frequencies are used for each technology. Certain frequencies are assigned to radio stations, others are assigned to cell phones, and so on.

---

geographic (jē'-ə-gra'-fik) covering a certain amount of the earth's surface

frequencies (frē'-kwən-sēz) the number of waves that pass a point in a certain amount of time

Student Cell Phone Owners at a Major University

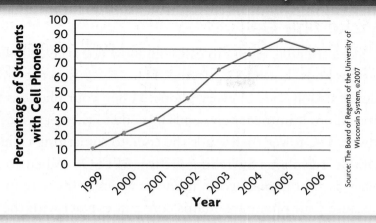

Source: The Board of Regents of the University of Wisconsin System, ©2007

The line graph above shows changes in cell phone use at one university from 1999 to 2006. **Think about what factors might have contributed to the huge increase in cell phone use over such a short time.**

Frequency Freedom

9   A **typical** cell phone **carrier** is assigned about 800 frequencies in an area such as a city. That might sound like a lot, but it's not very many at all when you consider how many people use cell phones. And add to that the fact that every cell phone call requires two frequencies at once: one for talking and one for listening.

10   Cell phone inventors have solved this problem by designing a system that allows them to reuse frequencies many times over. They take the total number of frequencies **allotted** to them and divide them up; some are assigned to one cell, some to another. And what allows them to get the most out of their frequencies is that the specific frequencies assigned to one cell can also be assigned to a different cell. (However, to make sure that frequencies from two towers don't **overlap,** cells right next to each other are never assigned the same frequencies.) Imagine that cells are set up like squares on a checkerboard—one square has an assigned set of frequencies, but another square a few jumps away might also be allowed to use those frequencies. This way the cell phone system gets maximum use out of a limited number of frequencies, allowing millions of people to use their cell phones at the same time.

carrier (ker′-ē-ər) a company that provides a particular service

Use Line Graphs

Study the line graph titled "Student Cell Phone Owners at a Major University." How much greater is the percentage of student cell phone owners in 2004 than in 1999? Fill in the circle next to the correct answer.

○ about 15
○ about 35
○ about 65

Ask Questions

Reread **paragraph 11**. What question would you like to ask about the information in this paragraph? Write your question here.

_____

_____

_____

How does asking this question help you stay interested in the text?

_____

_____

Make the Call

11   Say a friend is trying to call you. How does the cell phone system know how to locate you? The answer is in the unique identification code in every phone. When your phone is first turned on, it immediately sends its code to the nearest cell tower. The tower then sends the code to something called a Mobile Telephone Switching Office (MTSO). When an MTSO receives your phone's code, it knows which cell you're in. Because your phone maintains constant contact with the tower it's connected to, and because the tower communicates with the MTSO, the MTSO always knows how to locate you when someone dials your number.

12   So when your friend dials your cell phone from her cell phone, the call goes to her local cell tower. The MTSO checks to see which cell you're in and sends the call to your current cell tower. That tower sends radio signals to your cell phone, causing it to ring. When you answer, your phone's circuit board (the set of computer chips inside your phone) gets instructions from the tower to open the two frequencies for your call. Your call has been connected.

The Handoff

13   But what happens if you leave a cell while you're on a call? Maybe you're talking to a friend while riding a bus, and you move out of one cell and into another. You don't have to worry; most likely, you won't lose your call.

Cell Tower Reception

Tower Reception Range

Signal Handed Off to Next Tower

Cell Tower

When traveling, your cell phone signal is "handed off" from the tower you are leaving behind to the tower you are approaching. **Think about what happens if you're on a call and you travel into an area that doesn't have a cell tower.**

14   Before you leave the range of one cell tower, your call is "handed off" to the tower in the cell you're entering. It's a bit like a relay race where the baton—in this case, the radio waves your cell phone is using—is passed from one runner to the next. So as long as you aren't traveling into an area with no cell towers, you can go for miles without losing your connection.

15   Things have come a long way from the basic telephone. Cell phones free people from having to look all over for a pay phone when they're out and need to make a call. They also free people from having to wait by a phone when they're expecting a call. And they allow people to go just about anywhere and stay connected.

Did You Know?

Each year more and more features are packed into smaller and smaller cell phones. In addition to making (and receiving) calls, many cell phones can now do these things:

• Play music
• Take pictures
• Play games
• Connect to the Internet

My WORKSPACE

Draw Conclusions

Reread **paragraph 15.** One conclusion you could draw from the text is that *cell phones allow people to go wherever they want without worrying about being out of touch.*

What clues or details from the text support this conclusion? Write **two** clues or details here.

1. _____

_____

2. _____

_____

How does what you already know support this conclusion?

_____

_____

_____

Self-Check

Look back at the question you wrote on page 92.

• Does the information in the text answer your question? If it does, what is the answer? If it does not, where could you look to find more information?

Write your answers on a separate sheet of paper.

Understanding What You Read

Fill in the circle next to the correct answer. You may look back at the text to help you choose the correct answers.

1. The caption on page 93 helps support the author's point that
   - ○ A. millions of people can use cell phones at the same time.
   - ○ B. cell phones don't need wires to make and receive calls.
   - ○ C. every cell phone contains computer chips.

2. Cell phones and cordless phones are similar because they both
   - ○ A. transform sounds into waves.
   - ○ B. need an identification code.
   - ○ C. have a very limited range.

3. The *cell* in *cell phone* refers to a small, roughly circular
   - ○ A. computer chip.
   - ○ B. geographic area.
   - ○ C. set of radio waves.

4. Which of these sends radio waves?
   - ○ A. a telephone wire
   - ○ B. a circuit board
   - ○ C. a cell tower

5. What is one effect when a signal is "handed off"?
   - ○ A. The cell phone cannot receive calls from phones that use wires.
   - ○ B. The cell phone user is not able to move between urban and rural areas.
   - ○ C. The cell tower informs the MTSO that the cell phone user has switched cells.

Score 4 points for each correct answer.
_____/20 **Total Score: Activity A**

Understanding Line Graphs and Drawing Conclusions

The line graph titled "Student Cell Phone Owners at a Major University" from the article is shown below. Study the line graph. Then use the line graph to complete the activities.

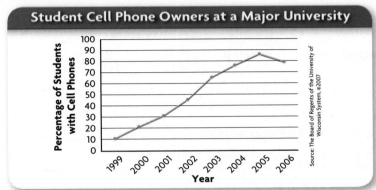

1. From the information in the graph, which of these statements is true?

   ○ A. In 2000 less than 20 percent of students owned cell phones.

   ○ B. In 2002 more than 60 percent of students owned cell phones.

   ○ C. In 2005 almost 90 percent of students owned cell phones.

2. Use the information in the line graph to draw a conclusion. Use clues from the line graph and what you already know to help you draw a conclusion.

   Clue from the Graph _____

   _____

   Clue from the Graph _____

   _____

   What I Know _____

   _____

   Conclusion _____

   _____

   _____

Score 5 points each for numbers 1 and 2.

_____ /10 **Total Score: Activity B**

Using Words

The words and phrases in the list below relate to the words in the box. Some words or phrases in the list are synonyms. They have the same meaning. Some words or phrases are antonyms. They have the opposite meaning. Write the related word from the box on each line. Use each word from the box **twice**.

transmit	**mobile**	**typical**
allotted	**overlap**	

Synonyms

1. issued as a piece of a larger whole _____

2. capable of traveling _____

3. go beyond _____

4. pass on _____

5. common _____

Antonyms

6. receive _____

7. leave a gap _____

8. taken away from _____

9. stuck in one place _____

10. unusual _____

Score 2 points for each correct answer.

_____ /20 **Total Score: Activity C**

Writing About It

Write Interview Questions Suppose you are going to interview someone who helped invent cell phones. Write a list of questions you would want to ask the person about cell phones. Begin each question with *who, what, when, where, why,* or *how.* Be sure your writing matches the information in the text. Use the checklist on page 119 to check your work.

1. _____
   _____

2. _____
   _____

3. _____
   _____

4. _____
   _____
   _____

5. _____
   _____
   _____

Lesson 8 Add your scores from activities A, B, and C to get your total score.
   _____ **A** Understanding What You Read
   _____ **B** Understanding Line Graphs and Drawing Conclusions
   _____ **C** Using Words
   _____ **Total Score**   Multiply your **Total Score x 2** _____
                                This is your percentage score.
                    Record your percentage score on the graph on page 121.

SEARCH ENGINES
The World at Your Fingertips

With a few keystrokes and a click
of the mouse, you can find all kinds
of information on the Internet.

READING SKILL **Reviewing the Reading Skills**

You practiced six reading skills in this book. Rate your understanding of each skill using the chart below. Use the following rating scale:

3   I understand this skill well. I use it easily and correctly while I read.

2   I understand this skill a little bit. I sometimes use it correctly while I read.

1   I don't understand this skill. I am not able to use it while I read.

Mark the box under the number 3, 2, or 1 for each skill.

	3	2	1	Need to review?		Turn to:
Making Predictions				Yes	No	Lesson 1, page 3
Making Connections				Yes	No	Lesson 2, page 15
Visualizing				Yes	No	Lesson 3, page 27
Asking Questions				Yes	No	Lesson 4, page 41
Line Graphs				Yes	No	Lesson 5, page 53
Drawing Conclusions				Yes	No	Lesson 6, page 65

If you rated your understanding of a skill at 2 or 1, look back at the lesson page where that skill was taught. The lesson page is shown in the chart above. Reread the skill definition and the example. This will help you get ready to complete the next lesson. After you have reviewed the skills, complete the sentences below.

The skill I find most helpful when reading is _____

because _____

_____

During this lesson, one thing I can do to improve my reading is _____

_____

_____

Getting Ready to Read

Think About What You Know

CONNECT Have you ever searched for information on the Internet? How did you do it? What do you know about how Internet search engines work? Write your answers here.

_____

_____

_____

Word Power

PREVIEW Read the words and definitions below. Then look ahead at the title and at the headings and images in the article.

imaginable (i-ma′-jə-nə-bəl)	capable of being thought about
generate (je′-nə-rāt′)	to create or produce
relevant (re′-lə-vənt)	related to the chosen topic
emphasis (em′-fə-səs)	special importance given to something
consideration (kən-si′-də-rā′-shən)	something that is thought about when doing a task or making a decision

PREDICT Use the words, title, headings, and images to make a prediction. What do you think the author will say about search engines?

I predict the author will _____

_____

because _____

_____

Reason to Read

Read to find out if the prediction you wrote above matches the information in the text. At the end of the article, you will be asked about your prediction. You will need to explain how your prediction is the same as the text or different from it.

SEARCH ENGINES The World at Your Fingertips

1   Maybe you're shopping for a new bike helmet and want to find the best deal. You could check stores nearby. Or maybe you have to write a school report about the Underground Railroad. You could go to the library to look up some information.

2   In either case, there's an additional option available. You can go online and pull up an **Internet** search engine, such as AltaVista, Yahoo!, Google, or Ask.com, and type the words *bike helmet* or *Underground Railroad.* In a moment, you'll see a list of **Web sites** on your computer screen that have information about the topic.

What's the Web?

3   One thing you should understand is that Internet search engines don't really search the Internet. They search a *part* of the Internet called the World Wide Web, or Web, which is the massive collection of documents and other materials that can be accessed online. (Other parts of the Internet you may already be familiar with are e-mail and instant messaging. To learn more about instant messaging, read *World Works, Level D*, Lesson 6.) The Web contains millions of pages of information on every subject **imaginable.**

4   It's great to have so much information available, but what happens when you need to find something specific? You don't want to go through millions of **Web pages** one by one. Imagine trying to find a book in the library if all the books were in a heap on the floor. Fortunately, librarians organize books on shelves and use a special numbering system so that you can easily find the books you want. Internet search engines do something very similar for Web pages.

Internet (in'-tər-net') a system of computer networks that connects computers around the world
Web sites (web'-sīts) locations on the World Wide Web
Web pages (web'-pāj-əz) the files containing information that make up a **Web site**

Imagine how hard it would be to find information on this messy desk. **Think about different ways information can be organized so it's easy to find.**

Connect
Reread **paragraph 4.** Use the information in the text to make a connection. Complete the sentence below.

When I read about how it's easier to find books in the library if they are organized, it reminds me

_____

_____

_____

because _____

_____

_____

_____

Ask Questions

Reread **paragraph 7.** What question would you like to ask about the information in this paragraph? Write your question here.

_____

_____

_____

_____

How does asking this question help you stay engaged in the text as you read?

_____

_____

_____

Crawl the Web

5 Maybe you've used a search engine before. You might not realize that most of a search engine's work is done before you even ask it to find something. While not all search engines work exactly the same way, they all need to gather information from Web pages and organize and store that information in a database before someone can do a search.

6 When a search engine does its first task—collecting information—it uses special programs called spiders. The search engine sends these spiders to visit as much of the Web as possible to collect information as they go.

7 Spiders start with a list of Web sites that the search engine company provides. Often these are the sites that tend to get the most visitors. When they visit a page, spiders **generate** a list of the words they find on that page and make a note of the page's address. Some search engines have spiders record every word on a page, while others want only the words they consider to be important, such as those found in Web site titles or those that appear numerous times on a page.

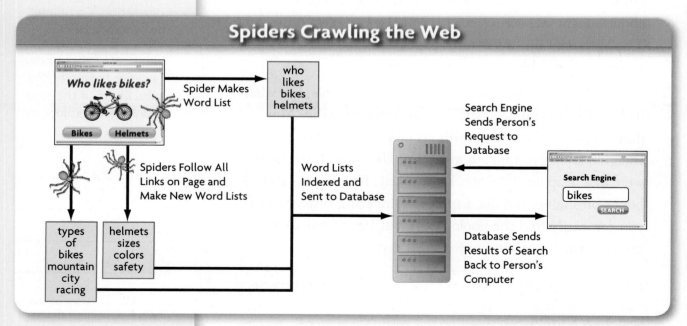

Spiders Crawling the Web

By following every link they find on a Web page, spiders manage to cover a great deal of the Web. **Think about why search engine companies would want to keep sending out spiders to revisit sites.**

8   You may wonder how spiders manage to explore Web sites that aren't provided in the search engine's original list. The answer is that spiders follow every **link** they find on a page. When they go to new pages, they build a list of words for each page—and then they follow every link found on *these* pages. They keep going until they have exhausted all the links on all the pages they visit. As a result, spiders crawl through millions of pages.

Excellent Indexing

9   If the search engine's work stopped with the spiders' word lists, it wouldn't help you much. This would be like assigning library books their number codes and then dumping the books back in the pile. To be useful, the information needs to be organized.

10 A search engine organizes the information from the spiders with a process called indexing. Different search engines index in different ways. Some may store just the word and its page's address. But many search engines factor in things such as whether the word appears in the title of the Web site and how often the word appears on the page. They also may consider whether the word appears in other links found on the site's pages. These all help determine how **relevant** a page may be to what you're searching for. These organized lists are then stored in the database, waiting for someone to do a search.

Where You Come In

11 Most search engine pages look very similar. There's a blank box where you enter keywords for your search, and there's a button that says something like "Go" or "Search" near it. After clicking the button, results appear within moments, showing a list of the Web pages in the database that contain the keywords you typed.

---

link (lingk) words or pictures on a **Web page** that, when clicked, take you to another Web page

My WORKSPACE

After typing in a few keywords, a person clicks a button like one of these to get immediate results. **Think about what some of the most popular Internet searches might be.**

Connect

Reread **paragraph 11.** Use the information in the text to make a connection. Complete the sentence below.

When I read about

_____

_____

_____

it reminds me _____

_____

_____

because _____

_____

_____

_____

My WORKSPACE

Use Line Graphs

Study the line graph titled "Search Engine Use on an Average Day in the United States." How many people used search engines in 2005 compared to 2002? Fill in the circle next to the correct answer.

○ almost half as many
○ almost the same number
○ almost twice as many

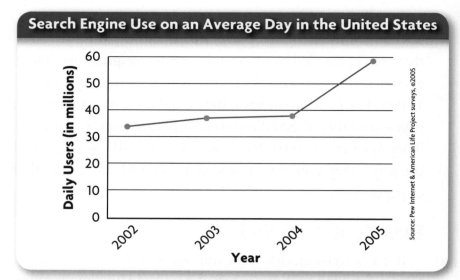

Search Engine Use on an Average Day in the United States

Source: Pew Internet & American Life Project surveys, @2005

More and more people in the United States use search engines each year. **Think about what some of the reasons might have been for the big jump in users between 2004 and 2005.**

12   The order in which the results appear is not random. A search engine orders the results according to how relevant it thinks each Web page is to your search. This is called ranking. Search engines may give more weight to some sites depending on how lists were indexed. If a search engine places **emphasis** on words found in Web site titles, the results at the top will likely be pages that include your keywords in their titles. If a search engine places more importance on how frequently a word appears on a page, the links for the pages where the keywords appear several times will appear at the top of your list.

13   Another factor that search engines often take into **consideration** when indexing and ranking is something called a meta tag. Meta tags allow site owners to determine which keywords they want their Web site to be indexed under. This can help site owners attract people to their sites.

14 Let's say a bike shop owner sets up a Web site. Instead of just hoping that someone will type in the name of her store, she may add meta tags that include keywords she wants associated with her site. For example, she may add meta tags for *bicycle*, *mountain bike*, and *bike helmets*, to name just a few. And if a search engine places emphasis on meta tags, there's a greater chance her site will have a higher ranking during a search using these keywords.

What Isn't Found

15 Because a search involves a database and not the Web itself, chances are search engines won't provide useful results about late-breaking news stories. Even though spiders are continually revisiting sites to update the database, it takes time for the database to catch up.

16 There are also hidden corners of the Web that probably won't pop up in a search engine's results. One reason search engines might not find these sites is because spiders never find links that lead to them. And if they don't find the link, the page won't be indexed.

17 Even though they don't turn over every stone in their search of the Web, search engines are still a great way to help you do many kinds of research, whether you're looking for a deal on a bike helmet, researching a history project, or trying to find out when a movie starts. Thanks to how they help you navigate the Web, search engines really do put the world at your fingertips.

My WORKSPACE

Draw Conclusions
Reread **paragraph 14.**
Using the clues and details in the text, what conclusion can you draw about how people and companies that sell things use the Internet?

_____

_____

_____

_____

How does what you already know support this conclusion?

_____

_____

_____

_____

Self-Check
Look back at the prediction you wrote on page 104.
• Does your prediction match the text? Why or why not?
Write your answers on a separate sheet of paper.

Understanding What You Read

Fill in the circle next to the correct answer. You may look back at the text to help you choose the correct answers.

1. Which of these sentences **best** summarizes the information in the "What's the Web?" section?
   - ○ A. The Web is like a library because it has millions of pages of information.
   - ○ B. Search engines help you access information on the part of the Internet called the Web.
   - ○ C. The Web contains so much information that it is hard to find exactly what you need.

2. The diagram titled "Spiders Crawling the Web" helps support the author's point that
   - ○ A. Spiders crawl through millions of pages as they search.
   - ○ B. Different spiders organize words in different ways.
   - ○ C. Search engines use spiders to collect information.

3. What problem with gathering information from Web sites does indexing solve?
   - ○ A. Spiders gather information but do not organize it.
   - ○ B. There are some Web sites that spiders may never find.
   - ○ C. Spiders visit many Web sites that have not been updated.

4. Because a search involves a database and not the Web itself, chances are search engines won't provide useful results about
   - ○ A. history projects.
   - ○ B. sites without meta tags.
   - ○ C. late-breaking news stories.

5. If you could choose another title for this article, which of these would be the **best** choice?
   - ○ A. What Search Engines Do
   - ○ B. Where Search Engines Look
   - ○ C. Why We Need Search Engines

Score 4 points for each correct answer.

_____/20   **Total Score: Activity A**

Understanding Line Graphs and Drawing Conclusions

The line graph titled "Search Engine Use on an Average Day in the United States" from the article is shown below. Study the line graph. Then use the line graph to complete the activities.

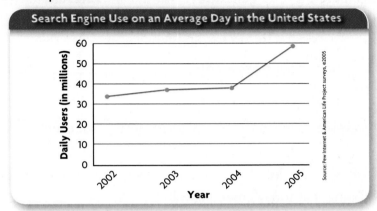

1. From the information in the graph, which of these statements is true about people in the United States?

   ○ A. More of them used search engines in 2003 than in 2005.

   ○ B. Fewer of them used search engines in 2003 than in 2002.

   ○ C. Almost the same number used search engines in 2003 as in 2004.

2. Use the information in the line graph to draw a conclusion. Use clues from the line graph and what you already know to help you draw a conclusion.

   Clue from the Graph _____

   _____

   Clue from the Graph _____

   _____

   What I Know _____

   _____

   Conclusion _____

   _____

Score 5 points each for numbers 1 and 2.

_____ /10   **Total Score: Activity B**

Using Words

Complete each sentence with a word from the box. Write the missing word on the line.

> **imaginable**　　　**generate**　　　　　　**relevant**
> **emphasis**　　　　**consideration**

1. This information about trees is not _____ to my report on flowers.

2. She has traveled so much that she has seen just about every place

    _____.

3. We are hoping that today's meeting will _____ some new ideas on how to raise money for charity.

4. The weather is an important _____ when planning a picnic lunch.

5. During the rock-climbing class, the instructor placed particular

    _____ on safety.

Choose one word from the box. Write a new sentence using the word. Be sure to put at least one detail in your sentence. The detail should show that you understand what the word means. Use the sentences above as examples.

6. _____

    _____

Score 4 points for each correct answer in numbers 1–5.
(Do not score number 6.)
_____ /20   **Total Score: Activity C**

Writing About It

Make a Connection Think about what you already know from your own experiences. This includes the books and magazines you have read and the movies you have watched. Then make a connection to the text. Finish the sentences below to describe your connection. Be sure your writing matches the information in the text. Use the checklist on page 119 to check your work.

When I read the information in the text about _____

_____

_____

it reminded me _____

_____

_____

because _____

_____

_____

Making this connection helped me understand _____

_____

_____

_____

Lesson 9 Add your scores from activities A, B, and C to get your total score.

_____ **A** Understanding What You Read
_____ **B** Understanding Line Graphs and Drawing Conclusions
_____ **C** Using Words
_____ **Total Score**   Multiply your **Total Score x 2** _____
                                 This is your percentage score.
                         Record your percentage score on the graph on page 121.

Compare and Contrast

You read three articles about technology in Unit Three. Think about the topic of each article. Then choose **two** of the articles. Write the titles of the articles in the first two boxes below. Draw pictures in the first two boxes that show how the topics are different. In the bottom box, draw a picture that shows how the topics are similar. Label the important parts of your drawings.

Title _____

Title _____

Both

Use your drawings to write a summary of how these technology topics are alike and different. Finish the sentences below to write your summary.

_____ and _____ are different

because _____

_____

_____ and _____ are similar

because _____

_____

Glossary

A

accumulate (ə-kū′-myə-lāt′) to collect a large amount a little bit at a time *p. 58*

acquire (ə-kwīr′) to get *p. 71*

allotted (ə-lät′-əd) given or assigned as a part of something *p. 95*

C

calculate (kal′-kyə-lāt′) to use numbers and math to find something out *p. 83*

characteristics (kar′-ik-tə-ris′-tiks) the qualities or features of something that are common to it and that set it apart from other things *p. 29*

consideration (kən-si′-də-rā′-shən) something that is thought about when doing a task or making a decision *p. 108*

consists (kən-sists′) is formed *p. 17*

consume (kən-soōm′) to take in by eating or drinking *p. 6*

controversial (kän′-trə-vər′-shəl) causing many arguments due to strong opinions about the topic *p. 29*

convert (kən-vərt′) to change something from one form into another *p. 8*

D

destructive (di-strək′-tiv) causing things to be destroyed *p. 58*

disrupts (dis-rəpts′) keeps something from continuing its normal activities or its desired path by creating a problem *p. 32*

distributed (di-stri′-būt-əd) spread over an area *p. 17*

E

edible (e′-də-bəl) able to be eaten *p. 46*

emphasis (em′-fə-səs) special importance given to something *p. 108*

equipped (i-kwipt′) having the things that are needed *p. 69*

Food

evacuated (i-va'-kyə-wāt'-əd) moved away from a dangerous place *p. 55*

exceed (ik-sēd') to be greater than *p. 58*

excess (ek'-ses') an amount greater than what is needed *p. 6*

exhale (eks-hāl') to breathe out *p. 69*

F

fatal (fā'-təl) deadly *p. 70*

fuse (fūz) to join separate things together so that they become one thing *p. 19*

G

gender (jen'-dər) the quality of being either male or female *p. 6*

generate (je'-nə-rāt') to create or produce *p. 106*

H

hazardous (ha'-zər-dəs) dangerous *p. 59*

I

imaginable (i-ma'-jə-nə-bəl) capable of being thought about *p. 105*

ineffective (i'-nə-fek'-tiv) not able to produce the desired results *p. 33*

infected (in-fekt'-əd) affected by germs that cause disease *p. 70*

intersect (in'-tər-sekt') to meet and cross at a common point *p. 83*

intriguing (in-trē'-ging) causing interest and curiosity *p. 43*

M

mobile (mō'-bəl) able to move around easily *p. 94*

monitoring (mä'-nə-tər-ing) carefully watching or checking a thing or situation to see how it changes over time *p. 85*

Nature

N

nutrients (nōō'-trē-ənts) the substances in foods, drinks, or chemicals that provide what is needed for growth and health *p. 6*

O

overlap (ō'-vər-lap') to extend over and cover up part of something else *p. 95*

P

predators (pre'-də-tərz) animals that survive by hunting and killing other animals *p. 43*

R

relevant (re'-lə-vənt) related to the chosen topic *p. 107*

ruptures (rəp'-shərz) breaks open *p. 18*

S

spheres (sfirz) ball-like shapes with all surface points at the same distance from a center point *p. 84*

sufficient (sə-fi'-shənt) as much as needed to suit a specific purpose *p. 19*

supplement (sə'-plə-mənt) something that is added to make up for what is missing *p. 44*

synchronized (sing'-krə-nīzd') made to happen at the same time *p. 84*

T

tolerate (tä'-lə-rāt') to put up with or allow something even though you don't like it *p. 31*

transmit (tranz-mit') to send from one place to another *p. 93*

typical (ti'-pi-kəl) having the special features of a particular group *p. 95*

V

vulnerable (vəl'-nə-rə-bəl) capable of being attacked or hurt *p. 47*

Technology

Pronunciation Guide

a	mat	oo	look
ä	father	ōō	food
ā	date	oi	noise
ch	chin	ow	out
e	wet	ə	pencil
ē	see	sh	sugar
i	tip	th	think
ī	fine	t͟h	them
ng	sing	ū	cute
ô	law	zh	usual
ō	so		

Writing Checklist

1. I followed the directions for writing.

2. My writing shows that I read and understood the article.

3. I capitalized the names of people.

4. I capitalized the proper names of places and things.

5. I read my writing aloud and listened for missing words.

6. I used a dictionary to check words that didn't look right.

Use the chart below to check off the things on the list that you have done.

√	Lesson Numbers								
Checklist Numbers	1	2	3	4	5	6	7	8	9
1.									
2.									
3.									
4.									
5.									
6.									

Progress Graph Instructions and Sample

You can take charge of your own progress. The Progress Graph on the next page can help you. Use it to keep track of how you are doing as you work through the lessons in this book. Check the graph often with your teacher. Decide together whether you need to work some more on any of the skills. What types of skills cause you trouble? Talk with your teacher about ways to improve your understanding of these skills.

A sample Progress Graph is shown below. The first three lessons have been filled in to show you how to mark the graph.

Sample Progress Graph

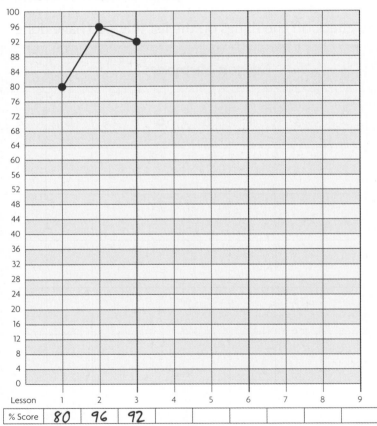

Lesson	1	2	3	4	5	6	7	8	9
% Score	80	96	92						

Progress Graph

Directions: Write your percentage score for each lesson in the box under the lesson number. Then draw a dot on the line to show your score. Draw the dot above the number of the lesson and across from the score you earned. Graph your progress by drawing a line to connect the dots.

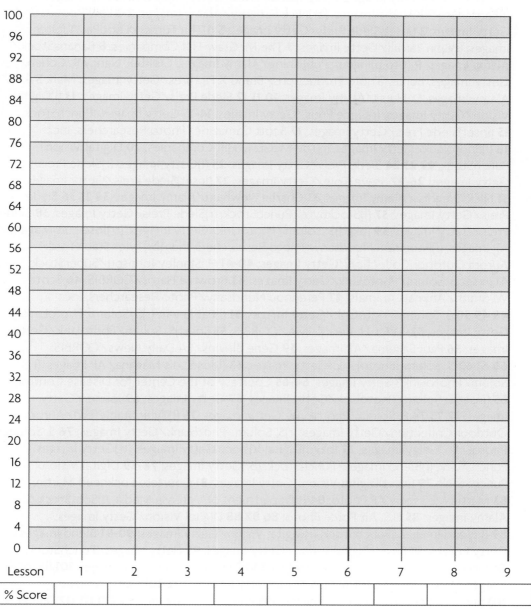

Lesson	1	2	3	4	5	6	7	8	9
% Score									

Image Credits